VICTIM

Of The

SWAMP

How The "Deep State" Destroyed
The 40-Year-Old Private

PATRICK BERGY

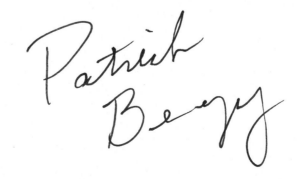

ISBN: 1977646468
ISBN-13:978-1977646460

DEDICATION

I have spent nearly the last 8 years overseas in Iraq, Afghanistan, and South Korea. I have 2 daughters; Mia, now 16, and Sarah, 14, as well as my 10-year-old twin sons; Bruce and James. They have all been without their birth fathers' physical presence for most of their childhood lives. Words cannot fully express the pain this has caused me personally by not being there for them.

I set out to make their lives better, and hopefully the lives of other American's, and their children, safer. In the end, I clearly fell far short of such a lofty, patriotic goal. Hopefully, when my children are older, they will be able to understand from this book why I made the decisions I did. We never could have imagined in a million years this would have, or could have resulted in such a devastating impact to our family. Their sacrifices, along with all children and family of service members, are the hero's in my story.

I am just a fallible father that always tries to do the right thing, and whom loves his children, and his country, with all his heart

God Bless the United States of America!

Contents

Preface

Victim of the Swamp is an autobiographical account of Patrick Bergy's decade inside what has become known as the "Deep State." I tell an amazing true story of my run for office in 2004, my enlistment at the age of 40 in the United States Army, and as a private military contractor.

This book is a deeply personal account of an average husband, father and Patriot that wanted to make a positive difference in his community, and his country. My documented attempt to protect democracy from the highest level of Florida's election officials will surprise you. My enlistment at 40 will touch upon your every emotion. My pioneering of social media psychological warfare as a private military contractor for the Department of Defense will likely leave you a little confused after reading the first two chapters - especially as it relates to the 2016 U.S. Presidential election. My fight to maintain honor and integrity from within the "Deep State" will hopefully enlighten you.

In the end, this fight destroyed everything in my life I set out to protect. I have done my best in writing this book, although I am not a professional writer. I have reached out to my elected officials with seemingly little incentive to act, as they don't want to end up like me, or are part of the systemic, Deep State problem.

This book is my final attempt to hold those accountable at the highest level of our government that violated our nations sacred trust. It is your duty as Americans, not as democrats or republicans, but as Americans that value freedom and democracy to help make a difference. I will never betray the sacred trust bestowed upon me with my Top-Secret clearance. I truly hope the carefully constructed knowledge I have provided to clearly support my claims, while maintaining this most sacred trust, inspires others. Had any less a Patriot been given the keys to the Deep State's kingdom I'm sharing with you now, America would not likely have the opportunity to fix it, which I have sacrificed so much for.

The illusion of trust and integrity in our government is being bought and sold daily by our elected officials, our military, and the military industrial complex like a commodities market. I say illusion because trust has been replaced with socially engineered psychological warfare, fraud, waste, and abuse.

To give you an idea how "inside" I was with the military industrial complex, I worked 8 years for a company owned by Obama's National Security Advisor, and former NATO Supreme Allied Commander; Retired 4 Star General James Jones. His son, Jim, was my boss at Dynology. I was contracted as a subject matter expert to develop pioneering applications in social media psychological warfare for the Department of Defense. Basically, I helped in pioneering social network "fake news" for the U.S. Department of Defense when social media was in its infancy. This application can provide complete covert anonymity to avoid any possible detection of Information Operations, and was truly capable of altering the outcome of an election, if so desired.

In laymen terms, if you wanted to fabricate, for example, the Russian's hacking the DNC with the intent to alter the outcome of our presidential election, you couldn't do it without having an application with the very same capabilities as those which I pioneered. Oh, did that finally get your attention?

What about the fact Obama's NSA owned and profited from military contracts while he was an acting NSA? That's crazy, right? Government oversight wouldn't allow such a conflict of interest to happen? Well, they did, and still do. Oh, and by the way, the leadership in our intelligence agencies Edward Snowden exposed for spying on American's inside the U.S., launched a new company designed to monitor American's in the workplace and provide employers with behavioral threat assessments based on your social media postings, banking, credit, criminal and driving history.

Once again, our leadership has seemingly taken the trust and integrity in our government they swore a sacred oath to protect, and traded it like a commodity for a way they can personally profit from. In the process, self-proclaimed "whistleblower," Snowden, has made it nearly impossible for our government, which at least had some oversight, to monitor for potential threats.

In November of 2000, I remember leaving my office at an online wholesale computer company I was working for in Tampa, and racing to the polling booth 20 miles away to cast my vote with just minutes to spare. I was furious to find out a few hours later that my vote might not have even been counted. Teams of lawyers from both sides of the political isle then fought their positions all the way to the Supreme Court. Florida's then Secretary of State, Katherine Harris, had been George Bush's campaign manager in Florida, and the Governor of Florida, the guy that appointed Florida's Secretary of State, Katherine Harris, was the presidential candidates brother. Putin himself couldn't have done a better of a job in destroying the integrity of America's election process if he had tried.

So, I stood up to defend what I saw as a direct threat to the integrity of our election process by running for the office of the Pasco County Election Supervisor four years later. I ran with no political affiliation because I didn't think the person counting the votes should hold a political obligation to any party. In what can only be described as one of the most partisan action possible, my opponent, a 6-term incumbent democrat, switched party's mid-way through his last term to Republican. Things like this seem to be such an obvious threat to election process and our democracy, yet good, intelligent American's go along without ever questioning it.

I will never understand why nobody ever said a word when $10's of millions in taxpayer dollars for new touch screen voting machines, were sent to a recycling center in Tampa to be shredded. Adding insult to injury, the shredding was ordered by my opponent, whom was Florida's strongest advocate for touch screen voting machines; running against my support of optical scanning systems. This is a truly amazing chapter which I hope may finally spark some debate.

Don't kid yourself with the time that has past, as most of these people are still in power today, and are never held accountable for their actions. My entire campaign was based on the stupidity of purchasing those very expensive touch screen voting machines, and trying to stop our county officials from wasting our money and threatening the integrity of our democracy.

How this all happened to me – a total nobody, is a picture-perfect example of what makes America the greatest country in the world today. All it required of me to participate in America's democracy, was the support of my family, and for me to get up off my couch, and stand up for our nations freedom, like so many that had before. This was only the beginning of what became a true calling for me. As a father, husband, and patriot, how could I just sit by and do nothing.

I spent several months of self-reflection following my run for Pasco County, Florida, Supervisor of Elections. I felt the best way I could help was with my knowledge and skills in computers. So, at the age of 39, I joined the U.S. Army Reserves, and that's when life started getting interesting fast. I saw something very wrong with our politics, and at a time our country should be coming together, what I saw was America becoming much more divided. Instead of sitting on my couch playing Monday morning quarter back and complaining about things, I thought that maybe I could help in being part of fixing the problem from the inside, so I enlisted.

It's now summer, 2005, and the millions of flags people had put on their cars after 9/11, were now mostly faded or gone altogether. As the death toll in Iraq and Afghanistan began to rise, support for our troops was still being preached from the pillars and pews, but few were stepping up to the plate and enlisting.

I couldn't just sit around while those that were serving and protecting our freedom, were dying. My friend and neighbor, Frederick Taylor, was a three-time Purple Heart recipient, and I had also grown to feel a great deal of duty to my country which I had not fulfilled. I wanted to help, and I truly believe in many ways I did. I also must acknowledge I became part of the problem for a brief time, as you will read later in the book. It doesn't help anyone to read my book and learn from my experiences, if I have not been critical and honest about myself in the process.

In the end, things came out terrible for myself and many of those I loved around me. I went from providing support to our national defense at the "tip of the spear," to struggling with homelessness and combat related PTSD for nearly two years now. When I say they have taken literally everything, I wasn't over-generalizing. Still, I maintain a small, fragmented light of hope and faith in America that keeps me from an even darker despair.

1   A Patriot Looks at 50

As I approached my 50th birthday back in the early fall, 2015, I realized how the events of my daily life today, all began shortly before the infamous attack on September 11th, 2001.

I was given the opportunity to go out on a date with a woman I had been in love with (but remained just friends) for about the previous 15 years. Her name was Lara Reading, and we got married about a year or so later, September 19th, 1999. Shortly after we got married, Lara became pregnant with our first daughter, Mia. I think it was just before Mia was born that Lara and I went to Disney World over in Orlando. I had been going to Walt Disney World here in Florida all my life. Even while growing up in Michigan, we went a couple of weeks each year.

Everyone that knows Disney World in Orlando, knows it takes about a year in advance to make reservations for dinner at Cinderella's Castle, so while we were there, I made reservations for Lara and myself for the following year, September 19th, 2001. My reservations at the castle turned out to be about 10 days after the attack of the World Trade Center on 9/11/01. Everyone was telling me, "don't go, don't go... Disney is a prime target for terrorists." To me, not going to the castle with my family would be a victory for terrorist everywhere. We went anyway, and it was the most amazing day I had ever spent at Disney.

In line that morning were about 100 people at the entrance of the Magic Kingdom – at most! The usual traffic at Disney in Orlando, I believe, is like 1 million people (don't quote that number, but it really is a lot.) We arrived at the castle with reservations made a year in advance, and there was only 6 other people in the whole restaurant. As nice as it was to be next in line at Space Mountain the whole day, it also served as a reminder of the fear, panic, and uncertainty that was bringing down our country.

I had a good job, nice home and was just starting out a family, but I also wanted to do more to give something back to my country. I was beta testing the new GE Centricity Electronic Medical Records (EMR) program between my employer, Florida Heart and Vascular, and University Community Hospital. After telling my employer I had enlisted, I was told my job would not be there for me when I returned. We filed suit the day I left for basic, and this too makes for a great chapter I think every employer should read. I was now in my life contributing to something good, but I always felt the desire and patriotic drive to do more for my country.

Fast-forward to 2004, and my now10-year background in computers and network security allowed me to see something that was happening in our election system which I felt was (and still is) a direct threat to our nations election integrity. That threat was the introduction of touch screen voting machines and election integrity following the 2000 election debacle in Florida. Literally hundreds of millions of dollars where being spent nationwide on new technology that had not been fully vetted. What testing had been done was largely by the industry itself, which had many top former election officials serving as directors on the board of voting machine manufacturing companies. I saw serious security flaws in the touch screen systems our local government and election officials statewide were endorsing.

I can't wait for you to read the details of my campaign in the following sub-chapters. It was an extraordinary event that only a handful of people even know ever happened, or likely cared. The outcome of the election, which ended in my very predictable defeat, resulted in the wasting of $10's of millions in taxpayer dollars on touch screen voting machines throughout Florida, which were eventually shredded and destroyed in a Tampa recycling center.

This book is not meant to be political. I actually have never held any political affiliation. It's not meant to be about me whining over spilled milk from losing my job for enlisting. It's not for losing my job as a defense contractor - for literally doing my job, although I must say that stung. This story is a uniquely accomplished perspective from someone that has witnessed first-hand how things work between our government, our military, and the military industrial complex. In Iraq, my talents helped in bringing together both Sunni and Shia for the first time in a thousand years. It was known as the "Al Sahawa," or "The Awakening." The most important weapon you can arm a society or culture with is tacit knowledge, and it is from this sharing of tacit knowledge with you in this book, that I hope to "awaken" American's as well. I hope you enjoy reading.

Saving the Vote

It was around November of 2000. Florida was the subject of international humiliation for its handling of the election between George W. Bush and Al Gore. The "dangling chads" and outdated punch card voting machines had turned Florida's election process into a sham. Florida's Governor, Jeb Bush, was the brother of Presidential candidate, George Bush. Our secretary of state, Katherine Harris, was the head of the George Bush presidential campaign here in Florida. This partisan relationship didn't help to instill much confidence or trust in democracy. I feel many politicians see our democracy as something they can use as a tool, while completely disregarding the damage it does to our nation. As is so often the case when our political leaders cannot instill public confidence through their actions, they just throw money at the problem. Making simple rules like not allowing the people who count the votes to have a political affiliation. Managing the campaign for someone on the ballot when you're counting the votes should have been an easy decision. Instead, they blamed the voting machines and throw taxpayer money at it (while complaining that our government spends too much money and is too big.) These people are somehow magically redeemed in the eyes of their constituents, and the voters just go about their daily lives. It may have worked on me as well with their solution to fix the election process by spending tens-of-millions of taxpayer dollars in Florida for touch screen voting machines. Fortunately, or unfortunately as the case may have been, I had too much knowledge in computers and network security, and saw through the political BS. I also had a grandmother (God rest her soul) and immediately pictured her with the same dazed look standing at a touch screen voting machine as she did trying (and failing) to use my smartphone.

The 2000 election debacle in Florida had its share of villains. Our secretary of state, Katherine Harris, ordered all the computers in her office to be re-imaged, resulting in the loss of all election related data and emails. Here in Pasco County, we also had a few rising stars in the race to destroy election integrity. In my opinion, Pasco's very own Supervisor of Elections, Kurt Browning, epitomizes the swamp life in Florida politics. Although not immune to the dangling chads, our election supervisor somehow decided the best way to show leadership and instill confidence in Florida's election process, was to switch parties from Democrat to Republican. For nearly twenty-four years he ran and served as a democrat. Shortly after being elected for his sixth term in Pasco as a democrat, he switches his party affiliation to Republican. To me, it looked like Kurt Browning had become the best Republican Election Supervisor money could buy. His timing was impeccable, as just that year the majority of registered voters in Pasco shifted from Democrat to Republican. Although Kurt publicly insisted this was not the reason for his sudden change of heart, a six-term partisan Election Supervisor is certainly going to be keenly aware of the shifting political winds.

Independent Candidate Strives to be Heard

I finally could not take any more of the idiocrasy I was witnessing, and decided to run for Supervisor of Elections in Pasco. I ran with no political affiliation (NPA), and refused to take donations from any political party, opting instead to use my tax return of only a few thousand dollars to fund my campaign. This did not go over well with my then wife, Lara, whom had plans to use our tax return funds to remodel our bathroom. I did, by the way, end up remodeling the bathroom myself, and it came out nice. I stood firm, arguing the position that democracy itself was in jeopardy and all she could think of is a new shower and toilet (Spoiler Alert: She was right.)

Figure 1 - Picture from Saint Pete Times article 11 Oct., 2004 titled "Independent candidate strives to be heard.

I went down to our elections supervisor office and registered my intentions to run for Pasco counties Supervisor of Elections, which was the easy part. Essentially, I was saying, "Hi, I'm here to try and take your job. Now, all I had to do is pay about $6,000 (the exact dollar amount I cannot remember,) or collect 2,312 signed petitions from registered voters in Pasco to make it official. Since my tax refund came to about twenty-five hundred dollars, it was time for me to start collecting petitions and hitting the campaign trail.

Wow, this American patriot was finally going to witness the political process from the inside out, and it didn't take long to get picked up by the local political radar. By the time I got home that evening, the head of the Pasco DNC, LaVaunne Miller, called me up (how in the heck did she even knew so fast I have no idea?) LaVaunne wasted no time asking me to switch and run as a democrat. I politely explained to her that I was running not to win, but rather on my personal values. She explained to me that just because she was a democrat, her and other democrats didn't need to vote for me. I told her that's what is great about this country, we are all free to vote for whomever she wants, and if the head of the DNC wants to vote Republican, she should go for it, then hung up on her. In an interview in the St. Pete Times, LaVaunne stated:

"Before he declared his candidacy, I spoke to him, and asked him to register as a Democrat," said LaVaunne Miller, who chairs of Pasco's Democratic Party... "Then the Democratic Party would be able to work for him. He decided against it, and I respect his decision."

Will the Democratic Party work to unseat Browning, the Republican incumbent? Miller responded: "We're going to support our own candidates." That is, Democrats."

For those of you keeping score, the democrat Election Supervisor just switched to the Republican Party, and the head of the DNC in Pasco was suggesting she and other democrats were going to vote Republican. Not because of my political positions, as she even didn't know what those were. The head of the Pasco DNC just wanted a candidate they could control. I am guessing Donald Trump knows a little about how that feels. I didn't hear much from her after that, and if memory serves me correct, the local DNC voted her out a short time later as the head of the Pasco Democratic Party. Her presence was nonetheless felt throughout my campaign, essentially encouraging democrats to vote for Browning. I didn't care, and even told the press in other interviews that I had no expectations of winning from the beginning. This was about trying to educate people on how stupid it was to spend seven million dollars on touch screen voting machines in Pasco. I publicly pushed the argument that the money would have been better spent on laptops for our kids in school, as an example. I think SP Times writer, Stephen Hegarty, said it best when asked about my decision to run with no political affiliation. Here is a quote from him in his St. Petersburg Times interview describing my decision to run with No Political Affiliation (NPA.)

"One of Bergy's first acts upon getting into the race was the political equivalent of shooting one's self in the foot," said Hegarty.

The Vote Bandit

I pushed on with the campaign and collected the required 2,312 signatures to get my name on the ballot. My platform was simple, yet complicated, based on trying to explain what can be very confusing vulnerabilities in touch screen voting machines in a way that voters could understand. With help from a friend, Cordes Owen; a brilliant web designer and subject matter expert in search engine optimization, I launched SaveTheVote.com. Others in the community like Janis Lentz, helped organize speaking events.

 My mascot was a cartoon rat that I created, (on left) that wore a bandit mask and carried a bag of votes slung over his shoulder. I called him "The Vote Bandit," and it was hilarious. My budget for this book only allowed for black and white inside pages, but the actual Vote Bandit was purple with a black mask. It didn't take long for me to get the attention of Kurt Browning, Pasco's current Election Supervisor. It was little consolation due to the fact I was struggling to get my message out, which was made abundantly clear in the "protest of one" picture of me you saw a few pages back from the St. Pete Times article, "Independent Candidate Strives to be Heard."

SaveTheVote.com did start to get some traction, and people were starting to follow the blog posts and updates I was putting on the site. In my first month, if memory serves me correct, I got about 6,000 unique visitors to my site. There was one "unique" visitor that kept showing up in my security event logs from a government computer, so I decided to do an IP trace and see if I could track down the IP address of my mysterious secret admirer. To my surprise, it was Kurt Browning. In about one months' time, my "Foe," (as the Times article called him,) Kurt Browning, returned to my site over 200 times. Here is a favorite quote of mine from the Times article;

"Patrick Bergy says his campaign Web site has received hundreds of hits from county-owned computers in recent months. He believes the traffic is coming from the office of his opponent, Supervisor of Elections Kurt Browning - a potential no-no because

public employees cannot use their office equipment for campaign purposes. "

I got a kick out of this because Kurt was publicly stating that I wasn't really a computer security specialist because I didn't have any formal college training. I busted his ass, so I guess I am not that bad. I collected the evidence and sent it to the Times and the Supervisor of Elections office, which prompted an immediate investigation into Browning for using government computers for his campaign.

Kurt had so many advantages being a six-time incumbent Election Supervisor. While I had to take time off from my job at Florida Heart and Vascular (without pay), to campaign, Kurt could do whatever he wanted with impunity on the taxpayer's dime. He literally did hundreds of interviews, most of which were on national news. With the well-funded support of Pasco Republicans, and likely even help from some in the DNC, he really didn't need to do anything but his daily routine to have an incredible advantage over me, or any opponent.

Before I keep rattling on, I wanted to remind everyone that my issues were never about Kurt Browning personally. I find many times people who don't have an intelligent argument to dispute what I am saying play the "hate card," making it seem like my arguments are personal attacks. This couldn't be farther from the truth. In fact, almost everything I have heard about Kurt Browning is that he is a good family man. He apparently did a good job from an administrative perspective as Supervisor of Elections during his nearly quarter of a century in that position. Well, that is if you were a democrat, while he was a democrat. If you were a democrat after Kurt switched parties back in 2002, then you would have most likely lost trust in your county Election Supervisor. If you were a republican during that 24 years, you would have likely questioned any call he had to make in a contested election because of his political affiliation.

My other issue would be that even though his chad had the least dangle compared to other Florida Election Supervisors, you don't send a bicycle repairman to fix a Ferrari. Kurt supervised the older analog voting machines, and the complexity of IT security, and other application development methodologies, is something you need to understand. The Implementation of an enterprise level network that our democracy relies on, is critical, and required a subject matter expert in the IT field. I dealt with such stupidity all the time working for the government, as you will read in later chapters. When you hire a subject matter expert in IT, then do the exact opposite of what the SME recommend, you're asking for trouble. Usually this happens because another company you scored as having a crap product, comes in and offers them a trip to Hawaii. You almost always end up with problems in situations like this, and why did you hire an SME in the first place? It's easier to teach an IT guy administrative stuff, than to teach an admin IT. Later you will read about my experience with USFK J8 in South Korea. This will really help you understand how this can become a very costly problem. Again, it's not personal with me, it's duty, honor and integrity.

I am reminded of a story from when I was in Iraq that explains what I mean. For a time while deployed in Iraq, I just gave up trying to fight all the waste. In this example, I was responsible for spending nearly $350,000 in taxpayer money because if our unit didn't spend the money, we would lose it in the next funding cycle. The only thing that $350,000 did for our mission, was made it possible for me to watch my hometown TV programs in full screen. I had previously only been able to stream in a smaller window on my monitor. I am serious! Yes, I know now this is a bad excuse. Had I not done it, I would have been replaced and sent home - unemployed. Spoiler Alert: That is how my career ends a few years later. When they come in and ask, "what do you need" to help keep our funding, everyone knows you need to find something to spend it on, or you will lose it next time. I know it makes no sense, but I am not sure I ever saw anything the government did that made sense. Maybe this is one of the reasons I like Trump? He doesn't always make sense, but at least he makes me laugh. As a successful businessman, you would never allow your company to run the way I witnessed our leadership managing budgets.

If Kurt truly had honor and wanted to do what was in the best interest of the county, he would have stepped down and recommended that someone with the proper knowledge provide leadership. I hate to say this, but if Pasco County taxpayers let these politicians get away with it, then Pasco county taxpayers get exactly what they deserve. When you see what happened after the election in more detail, you will see that is exactly what they did. I'm just laughing my ass off (while crying inside). Nobody tried harder than me to warn them, but as the old saying goes, "you can take a horse to water, but you can't make it drink."

There were really two main issues I ran on. They were best described as follows by Times writer, Stephen Hegarty.

Stephen Hegarty, "* Issue No. 1: Bergy doesn't trust Pasco's new touch-screen voting machines. As a man who makes his living working with computers, Bergy said the machines are nowhere near as safe and reliable as Browning insists. The lack of a paper trail troubles him."

It's sad, really, how our country is currently so mired down with investigations into the possibility Russia launched a cyber-attack on our voting infrastructure. There is really no legitimate reason for it if our leadership were not so corrupt and did their jobs. Tens of millions in dollars was spent here in Florida for electronic voting machines by Jeb Bush. The systems he chose went against the recommendation of the very select task force Jeb Bush created to determine the best, most secure solution. A couple of years later and Jeb is gone, but Floridian's got stuck with the bill when the touch screen systems he chose were sent to a recycling center and shredded. Ever more saddening is that the Florida Secretary of State that ended up ordering the touch screen voting machines shredded, was my opponent, Kurt Browning! You know, my opponent that was advocating for touch screen voting machines, the systems that were NOT recommended by Governors Select Election Task Force. Is this just a game to these people? It's like a race to see who can destroy America's election integrity the fastest. Russia can't hold a candle to these folks. My IT security background allowed me to see right through it, and my patriot blood was boiling.

Avi Rubin, Director of Information Security at John's Hopkins University, had demonstrated numerous ways ES&S voting machines could be hacked without anyone ever knowing. After reading one of Avi's whitepapers, I found an additional vulnerability he hadn't even noticed. I emailed him with what I found and he replied to confirm my findings. I understood many of the vulnerabilities inherent with the voting machines, how actual voters felt, and what was needed to bring back the integrity to our election process. I felt Pasco was completely on the wrong track choosing touch screen voting machines. For one, they don't leave a paper trail, so if you need to do a recount, it is performed by just hitting print twice. You look at the two separate printouts and that is it. The problem with this is the system had proven vulnerabilities in the both the system code, and in the hardware. No, I am not going to take you into a long and drawn out IT security lesson right now. Suffice to say there are any number of ways you can get malicious code into the voting machines to alter the outcome of the election. Ask Iran if they thought there was any way someone could get malicious code into their "air-gapped" nuclear power plant, meaning it had no physical connection to the internet. When you alter an election by altering the inside of a touch screen voting machine, hitting print twice is not going to get you different results. A paper trail, like what you have when you use a Mark-Sense optical scanning machine, automatically records the votes from the paper cards voters completed in the privacy of their booth. It does the same thing touch screen machines do by allowing you to report the results almost immediately, but if someone were to have altered the computer code or hardware, you could go back and recount the paper ballots manually if tampering was suspected. I was out there, meeting with and talking to the voters, and a paper trail was one of their biggest issues. It makes me sick how Kurt Browning and Jeb Bush totally ignored their own Election Task Force recommendations. There are no words to describe how I feel that they would ignore the clear wishes of their constituents. This is something I believe Charlie Crist saw immediately when he became Governor. He's my congressman now, and I have a lot of respect for him with that. Look around at all the players at that time the pushed Florida to go with the touch screen voting machines. The former Florida Secretary of State was not only a lobbyist for the voting machine industry, she was being paid by the companies she was recommending. So, when you try to make sense of how voters could be so ignored, look no further than the swamp at the local level of government.

Alter an Election with A BB Gun?

I took a trip to Fort Myers to document a vulnerability I had not heard anyone focus on with touch screen voting machines. The beauty was in its simplicity. It was right after hurricane Charlie tore through South Florida, leaving a wake of devastation in its path, along with a whole bunch of useless touch screen voting machines with no power, and election officials with no plan. I packed up my car with as much bottled water as I could fit, charged up my camera and headed to the office of the Supervisor of Elections in Fort Myers. I dropped the water off at one of the shelters on the way. When I arrived at the Election Supervisors office I walked inside to find what appeared to be hundreds of touch screen voting machines lining the hallway. I approached the lady at the front desk with my camera and began to ask her some questions. The most obvious was how they were planning to handle the election in a few days with no power to run the touch screen voting machines? This was a vulnerability I had published several months back when I noticed none of the voting precincts had any backup generators. The size and cost of even trying to place generators at the polling stations that were large enough to power anywhere from twenty-five to fifty touch screen voting machines in the event a precinct lost power would have been in the millions. I argued that a few well-placed shots with a BB gun in a largely democrat or republican precinct could effectively alter the outcome of an election by turning people away from the polls. When I asked the lady at the election supervisor's office what they were going to do without having power in the entire county for their local elections in a few days, she shrugged her shoulders and said, "paper ballots?" To which I sarcastically replied, "luckily you guys spent millions of dollars on these fancy touch screen voting machines to replace the paper ballots you had before". If memory serves me correct, this would have been the first actual use of touch screen systems in their county, and all those ES&S machines they had purchased for more than seven thousand dollars each were just lying dormant on the floor, waiting for the next election where the weather was more cooperative.

This is just basic common-sense people. Even if there was never any real likelihood someone would alter a touch screen system, or take out the power in a precinct, why not just have a paper backup anyway? The reason Pasco and the Secretary of State didn't want you to be able to do an actual recount is that they wanted to ensure never again to have a situation in Florida where there could be a recount. I was also informed they were concerned about access to voting machines for the blind, but that hardly required making all the systems touch-screen. They simply ignored the fact that their solution was not the more secure, reliable, or trusted by the voting public. It's all about feeding the swamp. They chose to line their own pockets with profits, rather than a common sense additional layer of security which would ensure voters the absolute highest level of trust. This is a perfect place segway into my next issue.

Trust (The Uday and Qusay Factor)

Stephen Hegarty " Issue No. 2: He thinks the supervisor should be completely free of partisan concerns. Bergy thinks Browning is not. He points to Browning's very public party switch from Democrat to Republican in 2002."*

Hegarty was one of the few reporters I found was quite fair to me. I found my experience with the main stream media to be very much the same as Donald Trump complains about.

Kurt Browning immediately became the darling of national media and the face of how the election process works. Kurt had it all figured out, the problem was not from a lack of trust in our political system, it was because voters were simply too stupid to punch a paper ballot properly. So, if we take away those annoying ballots that leave a paper trail which allow for a physical recount of votes in those closely contested elections, we wouldn't have anything to recount, and the problem would be solved. The greatest thing about Kurt's plan was that it would only cost the taxpayers of Pasco county about seven million dollars to replace all the voting machines we had used and trusted for decades, by choosing the new touch screen machines that didn't leave a paper trail. Sure, these new systems have numerous security vulnerabilities and exploits, but we would never know even know if someone did exploit one of these many vulnerabilities and altered an election. It seemed to him the perfect solution. Much like if a tree falls in the woods and there is nobody to hear it, does it make a sound? No more messy elections, plus you get a lot of twinkly lights and a computer screen you could touch with your finger. The voters of Pasco could not have been happier, but what they were being fed was all just lies from the swamp critters, in my opinion.

But what touch screen voting machines should Pasco go with? There are so many to choose from and so much money to spend. How can we decide? That's when Browning turned to the former Florida Secretary of State (turned paid ES&S voting machine consultant) to help decide which system to go with. Spoiler alert, she recommended ES&S. A steal of a deal if I ever heard of one. Statewide we purchased touch screen's for more than 70 million dollars, many of which got stripped down and sold for scrap or "crushed to bits" and sent to a landfill. Some of the original vendors offered Kurt to buy them back for a dollar each, but Kurt stood strong and refused such a ridiculous offer, opting instead to have them stripped of usable parts at pennies on the dollar, then shredded the rest into recycling material. What remained was buried in a landfill. Some were resold to third world countries. I mean seriously, people. we can't trust them, so let's send them to some warlord so their people can have democracy? This was all done on the orders of my opponent, Kurt Browning, after he was tapped as Secretary of State just a few months after he won the Supervisor of Elections race against me. On Kurt's orders, all touch screen machines in Florida were banned, and ordered to be replaced with, yes, I think you guessed it, optical scanning machines. You know, the machines I based my campaign on trying to warn Pasco that Kurt didn't have a clue as to what he was talking about.

Kurt is now my children's school superintendent, because what is more logical to ensure our children get the best possible education, than to have, in my opinion, one of the most failed government officials in Florida's Election Supervisor history, responsible for our counties entire school system. You know people, I couldn't make this up, it is simply too easy to verify by Times and Tribune reporting. It was the beginning of my personal victimization by the swamp. There have been more stories done about the touch screen voting machine ban debacle than I can possibly list. In most everyone I could find, they interviewed Kurt Browning. Sadly, all news stories reporting on this from our main stream media left out my part in this story. The part where I stood in front of local grocery stores with my daughters to collect 2312 signature petitions to get my name on the ballot. Where I was trying to warn everyone how stupid this was and what it would cost my county and our state. This was the best part of the entire story. The part where an average American gets off his couch to try and make a real difference. News organizations around the country still went with most all official comments to their hometown election hero and sweetheart, Kurt Browning, even as Congress was moving to ban touch screens nationwide. Did anyone reporting on this bother to check the tape from my one and only debate with Kurt Browning during the election? That would have been awesome. Maybe read the minutes back from the town hall meeting we had in Pasco where I was pleading to Kurt Browning and Mike Fasano not to waste our taxpayer dollars on touch screen systems? Kurt Browning was the president of the Association of Supervisor of Elections in Florida, and was pushing all counties in Florida towards the touch screen voting machines. There were six counties in Florida that still owed more than $33 million dollars when they had them "mash to bits," as was reported. I wasn't able to find the final numbers on what Florida actually got back from the purchase of 10's of millions of dollars in touch screen voting machines, but I would love to know. Does anyone think maybe Kurt should have been held responsible for millions and millions of dollars in fraud, waste, and abuse? Mike Fasano, a powerful republican political figure in Pasco County, literally jumped on stage at a town hall meeting about what voting machines to purchase for Pasco, and took the microphone away from long time democrat turned republican, Kurt Browning. This is where the swamp begins, at the local level. I was questioning Browning on the vulnerabilities inherent to the touch screen systems and how people wouldn't trust a system that didn't have a paper trail. Mike got so defensive and angry with me he started shaking. Mike was like a mother hen protecting her chick. How did they explain themselves to the taxpayers of Pasco for the machines they mashed into pieces just a few years after the purchase? How did they explain themselves for being responsible for wasting another couple million bucks to replace them with new optical scanning machines?

My Final Election Thoughts

To finish this retrospective of my first and (likely) last run for office, I hope everyone knows that nothing has changed in Pasco's county government, or at the state level. These people forget the fact the position they hold is not about them. It is about the office and what that sacred oath of office represents. During my campaign, I called having partisan election officials the "Uday and Qusay factor." I named it in honor of Iraq's Supervisor of Elections; Saddam Hussain's sons. I didn't pull any punches then, and if you follow my Twitter feed, @pfc40book you will see I still don't. Seriously, I was Trump before Trump was Trump. I believe American democracy should be more than that of Iraq under the Hussain regime when it comes to trust. After my failed political run for Pasco County Supervisor of Elections, I decided if I couldn't help fixing America's election system, maybe I could help fix Iraq's, post Uday and Qusay? This takes us to the next chapter, and my enlistment in the United States Army. Hooah!

2   Honey - I Want to Join the Army

This chapter is a riches to rags story, and chronicles my experience as a 40-year-old man struggling through boot camp, and my deployment to Afghanistan in uniform to serve at "the tip of the spear" for U.S. Central Command.

I had been working the last few years for a heart clinic in Tampa called Florida Heart and Vascular as the network administrator. I was tasked with converting the clinic from paper charts to electronic medical records and maintaining HIPAA compliance. I had a pretty good life with a nice home, beautiful and loving wife and two beautiful daughters that were two and four years old at that time. My 40th birthday was fast approaching and I found myself closely following the wars in both Iraq and Afghanistan on the news when I would get home from the office. I also remember watching hurricane Katrina devastate New Orleans on the news. I was so impressed with the troops that went in to help restore order and bring food and supplies to the victims.

My neighbor, Frederick Taylor, was a three-time Purple Heart recipient in Vietnam. Fred is a man I truly respect and admire, and I saw these things missing when I looked at myself. I didn't have a huge desire to get shot 3 times, but you get my point. How were my children going to look at me when they grow up, and what kind of an example was I going to be to them working 9-5 as an IT guy with a two-hour daily commute? I wanted to be more!

Although I had tried to enlist with my friend Randy around the time I was seventeen or eighteen years old, the recruiter felt we had cheated on the test because we both got almost the exact same score. We were both stoned most of the time back then, and the recruiter may have just used cheating as an excuse to boot us from his office, because we hadn't cheated. Looking back, I can't say as though I would have blamed him, but our hearts were in the right place. Now fast forward to the year 2005, when enlistment was down by record levels due to the U.S. fighting on two fronts in both Iraq and Afghanistan. They weren't throwing anyone out of the recruitment office. I saw media reports of recruiters going around to impoverished school districts to recruit underprivileged kids. These people were standing up to fight, many paying the ultimate price with their lives to defend this great nation that has provided myself and my family so much opportunity.

I don't exactly remember how the conversation went, but I approached my wife Lara and asked her what she thought about me wanting to serve my country. I felt that even though I was old, I had a skill with my computer background that would be useful. I asked for her permission, and her support, to go speak with a recruiter. Much to my disbelief, Lara was supportive of this and said if it was something that I felt strongly in my heart to do, that she would support me in this decision. I think she thought the Army would ever take me at thirty-nine years old, and she would have been right at that moment. I went down to the recruiter's office and told them I wanted to enlist in the Army. They were grateful for my offer, but regrettably informed me that the age limit for the Army reserves was thirty-five years old. They must have gotten a pretty good laugh after I left, as I was a computer nerd that was thirty plus pounds overweight and seriously out of shape. Don't just gloss over that last comment, I was seriously out of shape.

Tampa MEPS

A few months later, around the first week in October of 2005, the recruitment office sent me an email to let me know that the age limit had just been raised from 35 years old, to 39. They noted that I was turning forty in December, and that if I was serious about joining the Army, I had to be on the bus to Fort Benning in one week. I went back to the recruiter the next day and filled out the paperwork. They took me to a track near the recruiting station in Tampa and tested me to make sure I met some minimum physical fitness standards. I don't know what standards they had set, but somehow their original standards had clearly been lowered. They passed me as being physically capable of basic training. I think maybe they saw in me how I was mentally prepared, looking past my obvious physical limitations displayed on the field that day.

I then went down to get a medical exam, which is not exactly the same for a forty-year-old man as it is for the typical 18 to 24-year-old military age male. I was greeted by an Asian Dr. at the Tampa MEPS facility, which is where you get your pre-screening medical exam prior to being shipped off to basic training. I don't remember his name, but he was always smiling and had clearly been working at that facility for a long time. He had to take a second look at his chart when I first walked into his office. I think maybe he thought I was in the wrong room or was just lost? I was greeted with a special test reserved for those that are 40 and in the military called the Guaiac exam. Initially I thought it had something to do with my eyes, but when he asked me to drop my drawers and snapped on his rubber glove, I knew this was not going to end well, even for a confident heterosexual such as myself. I was correct in this assumption and will spare those reading this with the details of what followed, but suffice to say it had nothing to do with my astigmatism.

Have You Ever Smoked Marijuana?

Moving on from the anal probe, I was told we were going to be answering a few questions. This translated to what I soon discovered was government speak for a million different questions, most of which could have no possible bearing on anything. I found it to be as anal retentive as the Guaiac, but if the government is nothing else, it is thorough. The Dr. went on to asking me about my past drug use, which began like this, "Mr. Bergy, have you ever smoked marijuana," to which I replied "yes." He then asked, "How many times have you smoked marijuana, Mr. Bergy." To which I responded honestly with "a lot, most of my life, but I largely quit a few years ago, shortly around the time my first child was born." He followed up with "would you say more than once," I responded in a somewhat dismayed answer of, "yes." He followed-up that question with, "More than ten times?" Which I respectfully answered, "yes, more than ten times sir." He then asked, "would you say more than twenty-five times?" My answers remained, "yes." He knew it had been since I was in high school because I told him with the first question, so I became concerned as to when this line of questioning was going to end, thinking to myself, "is this guy going to walk this question up to what is likely ten thousand times I had smoked weed since high school?" I wanted to ask him what he was smoking before beginning this line of questioning, but much to my relief he continued in increments of ten and then stopped and simply noted my consumption as being, "more than one hundred times" in my records. As further self-incrimination would not add additional context to this story, and it will likely be read by my children someday, I will close out recounting my visit to the Tampa MEPS facility by noting I passed my medical and move onto the next step, which was the ASVAB.

The ASVAB

The Armed Services Vocational Aptitude Battery, otherwise known as the ASVAB, is what the military uses to determine what MOS, or Military Occupational Specialty you are qualified for. The exception to this would be driving a gas tanker in Baghdad, which in 2005 became the MOS of choice for those busted for substance abuse or drinking and driving, but wanted to remain in the Army. At least this was how it was explained to us during basic training, but they may have just been trying to scare those jacked up soldiers in my unit. To this day I am not entirely sure if our drill sergeants were serious or joking, but as you will read later, they are not really known for their sense of humor.

I think when you're younger, taking a test that will determine what your occupation will be in the Army is not a big deal. The lack of interest that I saw with most of new recruits taking the test seemed to support my hypothesis. When you're forty and have a family, career and a mortgage, this test is important. I was really stressing about this, but much to my surprise I scored exceptionally well. I believe my score was around 124 if memory serves me correct. Anything above 90, and you can pretty much have you pick of MOS. This score also supported my claim earlier in life that we didn't cheat when Randy and I had been rejected by the Army because we both did do so well. I chose the MOS of 25C, which is a signal support specialist, also known as an Information Management Officer (IMO). The story of Patrick Bergy is not like that of one of the greatest American patriots that ever put on the uniform, pro football player Patrick Tillman. That Patrick left this amazing career in the NFL, and was subsequently killed in combat in Iraq. I am not that Patrick, and don't even pretend to be. In many ways, I was inspired by hero's like Patrick Tillman and Frederick Taylor, but I like to think that along the way I have inspired a few people myself as Patriots in their honor.

Bound for Boot Camp, He's Booted From His Job

The following is taken from excerpts in the Saint Petersburg Times article titled "Bound for boot camp, he's booted from his job." It was published on October 27, 2005.

By CANDACE RONDEAUX
Published October 27, 2005

"A newly signed Army reservist claims a clinic fired him because of his enlistment. If that's so, it's a violation of federal law."

"TAMPA - He knows it's risky. At 39, he's not a young man anymore. He's got two little girls, a loving wife, a nice house in New Port Richey. And until he decided to enlist in the Army Reserves a few weeks ago, Patrick Bergy says, he had a good job."

I did have a good job. I liked the people that I worked with and respected them very much. Florida Heart and Vascular Associates, (FHVA), office manager Jennifer Law, called me up one day when I was doing sales and support for TCWO; an online computer wholesale company. FHVA's network administrator had quit some time back, and their server had finally crashed. Jennifer had called TCWO and I had randomly pulled her call from the phone queue. FHVA had purchased memory from us several months back, and she was hoping to get someone to help get their server back online. She was using the warranty from a couple of memory sticks to help repair an entire Microsoft Server at their clinic. This, of course, was in no way covered under the warranty for a stick of memory, but I decided to help her out anyway, and asked her to describe the problem they were experiencing. I easily diagnosed what the problem was and told her what to do. She did it, which fixed the problem temporarily, but the server was running out of space, and would likely have crashed again soon without immediate attention. Jennifer was very grateful that I helped her, when I clearly didn't have to, and likely even shouldn't have. If something had gone wrong, TCWO could have been liable. She asked me if I would be interested in coming to work for their heart clinic as their in-house IT guy. I went home and spoke with my wife, Lara, as this was a very big decision. We both prayed about it and decided that I should go down and speak with Jennifer further. It seemed like a great opportunity, so I accepted their offer. It turned out to be a great decision, as the .com financial disaster was just beginning, and TCWO ended up going out of business a short time later.

Working at FHVA was great. Drug companies would come in nearly every day and cater the entire staff with the most delicious lunches. I was quite happy with my job, and it provided sufficiently for my family, which is really all that mattered to me. What happened following my initial notification to FHVA of my intent to enlist in the Army was very disappointing, as was quoted by me in this excerpt from the article in the Saint Petersburg Times.

"But that changed early this month, according to a federal lawsuit Bergy filed Wednesday against his employer, Florida Heart & Vascular Associates, a Tampa cardiology clinic. The former computer network administrator claims he was fired after he told his employer he had enlisted in the Reserves.

The lawsuit claims that Bergy's boss, Dr. Kevin Klein, told him he was "stupid" for wanting to jeopardize his life by joining the military.

"It's called putting country before company," Bergy said in an interview. "But Dr. Klein doesn't seem to believe in that. He's putting company before country."

I was concerned that they would not be happy with me leaving, as we were right in the middle of a conversion from FHVA's existing paper charting, to electronic medical records, or EMR. My concerns turned out to be well founded. I went and sought the legal advice of Mr. Florin, an attorney with the law firm of Florin and Roebig, which specialized in employment law. We filed a Federal Lawsuit against Florida Heart and Vascular for wrongful termination. I believe it was filed under USERRA, which protected the military by Congress under the Soldiers and Sailors Act. I discovered that this was not as uncommon of a problem as I originally thought, and was surprised to find many companies try to fire their employees while they are deployed overseas. I learned also after returning from basic that it was very difficult to get another job while in the reserves. This was largely due to the possibility of multiple deployments, and employers preferring to avoid the problems. The Times came out to my home literally on the day I was preparing to deploy for basic training and interviewed me about the lawsuit that was filed. I was quoted in the following Times article addressing the Federal lawsuit and describe how I had tried to accommodate my employer.

"...But that changed early this month, according to a federal lawsuit Bergy filed Wednesday against his employer, Florida Heart & Vascular Associates, a Tampa cardiology clinic. The former computer network administrator claims he was fired after he told his employer he had enlisted in the Reserves.
"The lawsuit claims that Bergy's boss, Dr. Kevin Klein, told him he was "stupid" for wanting to jeopardize his life by joining the military. "It's called putting country before company," Bergy said in an interview. "But Dr. Klein doesn't seem to believe in that. He's putting company before country."

The conditions of my settlement with FHVA prohibit me from discussing it, so the best I can do in this book is show you excerpts from published news articles. Everyone has their own reasons for wanting to enlist in the Army. For some, it's enlist or go to jail, and I saw that a lot during basic. I didn't see many examples personally of this policy providing a higher quality recruit. In fact, I saw most of these jacked-up soldiers as a distraction to those Patriots that wanted to be there, like myself. For me, there was a lot of reasons that led to me enlisting, but whatever the reason, the least your employer can do is support you. I am not going to say I went about this whole thing as well as I could have, but I was right in my concerns with approaching my employer. As it turned out, when I did tell FHVA of my intentions, they responded poorly, in my opinion. I handed the case off to my attorney, and then I was off to basic training at Fort Benning.

As for the swamp, basic training was likely the only place I found it to be virtually non-existent at the command level. From our drill sergeant up, there was zero tolerance for what many describe as "institutional racism" or fraud, waste, and abuse. Of course, there were small groups or individuals which sought to game the system, but if you had the guts to speak up if you saw something wrong, you were supported at every level of command.

When I arrived at basic training on October 28, 2005, I was told two other guys that were thirty-nine were in the process of completing basic, and that one of them had just done an interview for a large magazine, the name of the publication escapes me. It is my understanding that I was possibly the first actual 40-year-old with no prior military background to successfully complete basic training in the history of Fort Benning, but cannot confirm that. I spent my 40th birthday doing the live fire, low crawl in the muddy Georgia clay. It was physically demanding, but not nearly as difficult mentally as missing both of my daughter's birthdays for the first time, which is what happened on around my second day at basic training. You're prohibited from using the phone for the first several weeks to call anyone during basic training. If not for the compassion of the drill sergeant (compassion and drill sergeant are words not often used together in the same sentence during basic training) that snuck me to a payphone, I am not sure I would have made it past the first few days at boot camp. Tears rolled down my face the moment I heard their voices, and the 2 minutes I was given that day on the phone was a mental recharge that lasted me the full 9 weeks.

Basic training at 40 for someone with no prior military service was not just new territory for me, it was new territory for the Army as well. The drill sergeants, I feel, likely cut me more slack than they did with the more demographically typical 18 to 24-year-old military age males. For the most part I was about 10 years older than my oldest drill instructor, or even most in my command apart from COL Powers. I had the pleasure of running into COL Powers in Korea about 5 year later and had a nice chat. I think he possessed a very good understanding of the dynamics at play with older recruits.

As for me, there was no going back to my old job at Florida Heart and Vascular; that bridge had been burnt. I think perhaps Dr. Klein's actions had inadvertently forced me to be all that I could be, as the old Army recruitment slogan went. Failure was not an option, but success was not a right, either. Successful completion of basic training was an honor and a privilege that could only be earned through blood, sweat, unimaginable physical pain and mental anguish. This is not some marketing line used in a recruitment commercial, it is the reality I faced as a 40-year-old man struggling to make it through 9 weeks of hell – let alone the first week of boot camp. In the weeks that followed, it only got worse. I don't have the exact numbers, but of the roughly 20 men I remembered that started basic training with me between the ages of 35-39, you could count on one hand the number that made it all of the way through. Few made it more than a few days.

Basic Training at 40
The Shark Attack – Day 1

You could feel the anxiety of the other recruits on the bus as we arrived at Fort Benning with our personal items. Some people didn't read the instructions prior to arriving and brought luggage, not understanding the additional challenges that would create in that first moment of your arrival. The initial arrival at basic training is affectionately known as "The Shark Attack." The bus doors open and drill instructors swarm the bus yelling and screaming instructions at a very rapid pace. As an adult, I had done some research, and found the shark attack to be much less frightening that what I was led to believe. I truly couldn't understand how so many people simply couldn't follow the most basic instructions they were given in the first few moments of our arrival. I am guessing it was mostly from the stress, but it was later explained to me that this moment is what basic training was all about. It was to break down a person's basic habits, like how you shower, brush your teeth, make your bed, follow orders, and respect the chain of command. To your average 18 to 24-year-old military age male, this is a challenge because many have not been properly taught these basic responsibilities. To a 40-year-old man, you should already know most of these things. There were exceptions, but those that didn't understand this, were the ones that were weeded out early in the training. Most of the kids that had enlisted as true patriots picked it up well, but many could never accept the strict compliance necessary to build a successful soldier, and those were weeded out early. By the end of the first day we had been introduced to our new quarters and instructors. We were then told about what to expect the next morning, the initial PT test.

The PT Test – Day 2

We were woken around 0400 hours (4:00 am) and went down to prepare for our initial PT test. Let's just say my initial testing scores where not that promising. We began, I believe, with push-ups. In this event I was told that to complete basic training successfully, I would be required to perform something like 42 proper push-ups, which didn't really look that hard to do. I went down to my hands and knees and prepared to complete as many push-ups as I could physically do in 2 minutes. The drill sergeant clicked his stop watch, said "go," and proceeded to count the number of "proper" push-ups I did as they were performed. He counted 1,….2,….3,….4,….4,….4. I stopped and looked up at him and asked why he had not progressed past 4, (actually, my wording was more like "what the f*%k?" which was entirely the wrong response, I can assure you.) He then explained I had not properly, "broken the plane" between my shoulders and my back, so I was only counted as having completed 4 actual proper push-ups. This concerned me, as my final number required for graduating basic training was about 38 more than where I was now, and I had only 8 weeks to get there. My disappointing performance continued with the sit-ups, as well as the 2-mile run. I did a few more sit-ups than I had completed with push-ups, but my 2-mile run was another, exceptionally disappointing matter entirely. My time to beat for graduating basic training with the 2-mile run was 18 minutes, 18 seconds. I came in just a little over my required time on my first run, to say the least. In fact, if memory serves me correct, they drove out in a truck and picked me up after about 30 minutes or so. My time had been explained to me as being just slightly greater than if an elderly woman walked the 2 miles.

We broke after that disappointing performance for my first breakfast, and after that had some more orientation.

I learned then we were not allowed to use the phones for any reason, and we were all told to expect this would be enforced for some time. I couldn't imagine how my daughter Mia, whom had just turned 5 that day, would feel about her father not being there on her birthday for the first time. My other daughter, Sarah, would turn 3 years old 2 days later as well. I tried not to show it, but inside I was really stressing out with all that was going on around me, and questioning my decision in joining the Army. With my kids and wife back at our home in Florida, I questioned my sanity on more than one occasion in the passing days, and as you will read later in my story, even years. I know the importance of discipline, but my drill sergeant knew my situation, and quietly took me down to the pay phones for a few minutes to wish my girls happy birthday. I explained to them it will be a while before I will be able to call, to behave, and listen to their mother. I could hardly speak from all the emotions going through me right then. It is even difficult for me to write about this now. I felt so much power after getting off the phone, that I didn't even notice the pain which had begun to set in after my first day of actual exercise in over 2 decades. I could never have imaged the increase in pain that occurred over the next few days, and 800mg Ibuprofen was the only thing they could give me for my muscle pain. It helped at first, but after about a week, Oxycodone would not have helped with the pain I was in.

As the weeks went by I questioned everyday if I would ever be able to meet the physical requirements to pass basic training. I was putting in my best effort, but the results were not showing much progress. One of the main tools in the drill sergeants discipline kit was group punishment. We were all paired with a "battle buddy," and we were expected to work together as a team. So, when your battle buddy was wrong, so were you, or in many cases, your entire squad. If your battle buddy showed up for a daily formation and was missing a required item, for example, their gloves, or being late for formation by even a few seconds, the drill sergeant would do what they called "smoke" me. Even though I was in formation on time and with all my required items, the drill sergeants would say "Bergy, drop and give me 5." This getting "smoked" meant I had to drop and do 5 push-ups, or whatever physically demanding punishment they saw fit. It was really embarrassing to me, not because of the discipline, but the fact they would tell everyone else to "drop and give them 20." Then one day, about 6 weeks into our 9 weeks at Benning, my battle buddie showed up late for formation, or some jacked up thing like that. There were like 300 soldiers in formation on that freezing cold Georgia morning, when either DS Jones or DS Dicks, I can't remember who, yelled out for me to "drop and give me twenty." My face lit up with proudest smile I may have ever made. I stood straight with pride at the position of attention and shouted back in absolute delight, "YES DRILL SERGEANT, THANK-YOU DRILL SERGEANT!" I dropped to the ground and knocked out my 20 push-ups. It was at that very moment I felt, for the first time since arriving at basic training, that I might just graduate after all.

Gracefully Surrendering the Things of Youth.

The title of this sub-chapter was taken from a poem called Desiderata. I find many parts of Desiderata profoundly prophetic. Passing basic training wasn't just about how many push-ups, and sit-ups you can do in 2 minutes, or how fast you run 2 miles. There is a mental component you need to manage when your day to day "social" routine is interrupted like it is in basic training. I had quit smoking nearly 7 years earlier, but it was hard on smokers, as smoking during basic is strictly prohibited. Your diet, from whole milk, to steak dinners, fast food, and coffee, are very hard things to quit, but to graduate, we also had to meet the weight requirements. When I arrived at basic I needed to lose almost 30lbs to meet my required weight to graduate, and had only 9 weeks to achieve this. I had to watch everything I ate during my training, while still being able to maintain the physical requirements necessary to graduate. The hardest thing for me to give up was without a doubt, coffee. I had been sitting behind a computer desk for the last 10 plus years drinking coffee and eating mostly things I shouldn't be eating. As the weeks passed, there were times that I would give anything for a cup of coffee, and to make matters worse, instant coffee packets were included in almost all MRE's, or meals ready to eat, which were provided to us out in the field. Every day I lived with the temptation to sneak that little packet of coffee from my MRE and have a cup, but I never did. Then one day in the last week or so of training, a drill sergeant walks up and quietly hands me a pack of instant coffee, remarking that he knew I must really miss having one of these. He said for me to go ahead and enjoy, you've earned it, but keep it quiet. There are people that have gotten multi-million-dollar bonuses from their companies that wouldn't appreciate this gesture and recognition of their efforts as much as I did with that single pack of instant coffee. Even more crazy is that I didn't even drink it. I could have, but there was a reason I wasn't allowed coffee. It is a diuretic, and can dehydrate you during training. Would this one pack of instant coffee have any discernable impact on me? Likely not, but I was taught a very valuable lesson back on my 40th birthday during what's called the live fire, low crawl, in the wet, red Georgia clay. No short-cuts!

The weeks in basic passed very slowly, but as I mentioned earlier, it was in the last few weeks that I began feeling I might just be able to pass this. Jumping ahead a slightly in the story timeline, I felt this would be a good time to tell one of the more amusing, positive interactions I had in basic training. We had a short break for Christmas, and returned to training just in time for my 40th birthday on December 30th. I decided that morning to treat myself to something special, a glass of milk! Although milk is not prohibited like coffee was, it is not something you should be drinking when you have as much weight to lose and physical shape as I did in such little

39

time. If a drill sergeant saw someone overweight drinking milk, they would say, "enjoy that, then go run 2 or so miles and see how you feel." So, knowing that, during lunch on the afternoon of my 40th birthday, I quietly made my way over to the milk machine at the DFAC. Just as I was beginning to pour myself this tall, beautiful, cold glass of milk, DS Jones walks up to me. He said, "you're a little old to be drinking milk Bergy, don't you think?" Such "old man" jabs were common, and I didn't mind the healthy ribbing at all, but this time I had a pretty good response. I stood at the position of attention and shouted, "NO DRILL SERGEANT, JUST TRYING TO PREVENT THE EARLY ONSET OF OSTEOPEROSIS, DRILL SERGEANT." He got the most puzzled look on his face, smiled, and replied "very well, Bergy, carry on then."

Managing Expectations

There seemed to always be a lack of respect for the institution itself by a handful of malcontents. Soldiers were prohibited from having cell phones, yet in complete defiance, some would be on their phones while standing in formation, which is something you should never see. New rules were limiting what options instructors had, which I adamantly disagreed with. There was also a shortage of drill instructors, which didn't help either. COL Powers felt strongly that the Army needed to change some of its older techniques used for discipline, and were becoming more considerate as to the welfare of the new recruits. I was initially opposed to this, again expecting my experience to be more like the movie, "Full Metal Jacket." Talk of "stress cards" that would allow a recruit to rest or get out of some sort of disciplinary action was not making our drill sergeants very happy either. I firmly believe that COL Powers was making the right call by reforming policies to encourage greater respect to the recruits, while still pushing them both physically and mentally to make them better soldiers.

I remember when I first arrived at basic training of an expectation of very strict discipline, from an institution that had been perfecting the process of discipline for over two centuries. Unfortunately, because of the same change in policy that now allowed a 40-year-old man to enlist in the Army, there was an even greater number of jacked up soldiers that had clearly been freshly scrapped from the bottom of society's barrel. "Join the Army or go to jail" options were clearly back and in full strength. The Iraq war had dropped enlistment to historic lows, and they were clearly taking anyone at this point (yes, I am a good example of them lowering their standards.) When the Army starts taking 40-year-old, out of shape nerds with prostate issues, standards have clearly gotten low. That said, 40-year-old nerds are not nearly as disruptive to order and discipline.

Rape, or Boys Just Being Boys?

President Trump recently made a controversial decision banning trans-gendered soldiers. My experience back at a time when "don't ask, don't tell" was in place should be considered. A preacher once told me that you cannot legislate morality. I tend to agree with this on a fundamental level. Forcing the military to allow openly gay or transgendered people, even with the best of intentions, doesn't end well. There are good and bad people in this world, and I live by people being defined by their actions, not their race, gender or any other label society claims to define someone as. In my first marriage, my two best friends in this world were also my "best men." Gay as the day is long, Martha Stewart would have been jealous of how well Calvin and Benson decorated our wedding. But in the military, you are recruiting large groups of people based on their pre-disposition towards violence. Anger management is dealt with by nine weeks of training these people to kill. In my opinion, it is the wrong place for a social experiment. Getting it wrong has consequences, but you be the judge with my next story.

A few small wannabes "gangs" started to form shortly into our first days and weeks at basic training, and the strong were starting to attack the weak within their pathetic little groups. I think it was mostly just to show those in their little "packs" they were cool, but also helped establishing dominance within their own little system. It made me sick with some of the things these thugs would get away with. The final straw was one day in the barrack showers a bunch of guys in this gang, (their gang name escapes me now, but it was the same name of our cold weather underwear.) The leader of this gang would pick on this one guy in our unit every day, but I won't reveal his name. One day it went too far when several guys "simulated" raping him while they were all naked in the showers. As he tried to escape, the others held him down. I use the word simulated very lightly, and would compare the mental images I remember of it to the images we saw in Abu-Ghraib prison. In my opinion, this was the worst possible humiliation a man could have suffered. The guy they did this to was a good soldier, and although you could never justify such an act, for sure this guy, unlike the guys that did this to him, was there because of his love of country and Patriotism, not to keep out of jail. Eventually, because nobody else would step up and defend him, I shouted out a few choice words telling them to stop, and they did. For someone like myself struggling to fit in and stay off most everyone's radar, it was a very uncomfortable position to take. Afterword's I wrote down the incident, and privately handed it off to our senior drill sergeant, who took it up the chain. Immediate action was taken, and the leader of the gang was busted out of the Army for it. Most everyone else involved lost whatever rank they had at the time, and were busted down to buck privates. Honestly, I thought at the time a few others should have been in trouble, but it seemed as though they used this second chance to make some big changes. I think some might have become good soldiers. It was amazing really. Since reporting that incident, I never had anything relating to fraud, waste or abuse I reported officially acted on. If a 40-year-old father wasn't there that day, would anything have been reported? I did not get the impression that this incident was unique, but did get the impression few would ever actually report it.

The Army regulations clearly prohibit even perceived gang activity. Our command included such behavior in our initial in-process briefings, if memory serves me correct. I don't remember them stressing the severity of the rule, but it was truly and quickly enforced. It appears a "mob rule" mentality has existed for some time. I think this would be an example of where the new policy allowing older men to enlist helped to improve the system. I paid a price for putting my neck out where many of these younger guys didn't feel it belonged. To my surprise, the clear majority of those in my unit respected me for what I did in reporting the incident, privately. That said, several others after that tried to make my last few weeks a lot more difficult, but their efforts were doomed to fail. I became friends with the guy they had been torturing in the showers. My command handled everything well here. The incident seemed to fade away quickly. I didn't have time for anything but focusing on meeting the physical requirements to graduate, and the final 12+ mile ruck march in full battle rattle that was awaiting me.

It was on my 40th birthday I had to do what was called the "live fire, low-crawl." This was performed under barbed-wire strung just a few feet off the ground while on my hands and knees for a hundred or so meters. Live, 60 caliber rounds being fired over my head, and I was near total physical exhaustion. I got to the finish line with just my last ounce of strength, and then rolled over the line, rather than continuing with the low crawl. The drill sergeant looks down at me and screams, "you don't roll across my line Bergy, go back 20 meters and try it again." I did it, and when I finished I was not angry at that drill sergeant for being some asshole like most of the younger kids did. I saw this as an incredible lesson about not quitting. You need to go the entire distance and give it 100% of your efforts the entire way, or you will only be cheating only yourself. We are being trained for combat, to kill or be killed. The ones that come back from combat missions, are the ones that didn't give up when things were their worst. This is what I thought of when handed the delicious cup of coffee by my drill sergeant in recognition of my progress a short time later. I didn't drink any coffee until the very end of basic training after completing the 12-mile ruck march.

The Final Ruck March

A ruck march in full battle rattle means all your equipment; including ballistic vests (with the heavy metal plates) and M15 rifle at low ready. I believe it is between 60 -80lbs? The march ends in a traditional ceremony, and was the final test of our endurance. If you dropped out of the formation in this final 12+ mile march, you would fail basic training and must start over. Starting over was not an option for me, and I wasn't about to let any of these jacked up meatheads get to me.

In the first few weeks of training, and I am guessing with the numbers here, it seemed to me like about half of the 35-39-year-olds had dropped out due to one reason or another. The numbers I am seeing reported now, in 2015, by the Army indicate the retention levels are about the same as the other age groups. I find that to be a surprising increase in retention, but again, I am just estimating by what I saw personally. I felt near death from muscle pain, and was going at least two or three times a week to the med center for 800mg Ibuprofen, and I was still in excruciating pain. Many times, I did not think I would ever make it, and I was not alone with this among those in my age category during my time in basic. I am reminded of our final test of endurance, which was required for successful completion of basic training, the 12-mile ruck march. I touched on this a bit earlier, but it deserves more discussion.

The ruck march had several hundred soldiers in formation, all wearing their full battle rattle. You have your ballistic vest with chest plate, your weapon and backpack, survival gear, food, water, and other essentials. You were also in your boots, not the tennis shoes we usually would run long distances in. All total it is over 60-80lbs. One poor soul got stuck carrying the SAW, which is a massive, high capacity weapon and very heavy, like the weight of 2 or more M4's. This 12-mile march takes about 2.5 hours, if memory serves me correct, and that includes 2x 15 minutes rest breaks to take a pee and hydrate. It's a grueling test of endurance, and you must keep in formation. If you drop out from the back of the formation, you would be required to go through basic training again. I somehow managed to end the march in the same row I began in, which was damn good. On my first 15-minute break I removed my shoes to find mostly all blisters, and my socks wrung with sweat. Pain was everywhere throughout my body, and the pace never slowed. By the second 15-minute rest, when I took off my socks and wrung out the sweat, it was bright red from all the blood. The blisters from an hour ago were now blisters, on top of blisters. With such large open wounds, I found myself in the last 20 minutes of the march walking only on the sides of my feet, still at a pace of nearly a ten-minute mile. By comparison, my best time running 2 miles was 18 min and 18 seconds (maybe a little less a few times), so going 12 miles at only about 1 minute per mile less than what I do my PT run at was not something I could have imaged myself capable of even a few weeks earlier. I still deal with the damage done to my feet on that final run, and they have never been the same since. When we ended the 12-mile ruck march and I stood before the rest of my brothers in arms that had also finally completed basic training at the same ceremonial site used for decades to signify the completion of basic training, I didn't feel an ounce of pain. I just stood there, awe-struck that this part of my military service was now behind me, and that I was now officially a soldier in the U.S. Army. Hooah! My wife and daughters, Mia, and Sarah, came out to watch my graduation ceremony, and it was a really great day.

Advanced Individual Training (AIT)

My next stop would be AIT, or advanced Individual Training. I can't really say I could even write a full chapter on AIT, as I tested-out of like 70% of the classes. I already had the required certifications from working in the tech industry for over ten years, so they allowed me to take the final exam at the beginning of each required class. As I passed each exam, I could go directly to the next class. I finished nearly 18 or so weeks of required courses (I don't remember exactly) in about 4-6 weeks, and was finished with AIT. They asked me if I wanted to stick around and graduate with the rest of my class, but staying for 12 more weeks doing nothing didn't seem like as good of an idea as going back to Tampa to be with my family. I also wasn't eager to join my first unit, the 810 Military Police. Yes, you heard me correct, I was not in a hurry to go to the 810 MP, because I was supposed to go to JCSE. I would only spend one weekend of drill duty as an MP at the 810. I processed in, then out-processed 2 days later before joining up with the Joint Communications Support Element, or JCSE, over at McDill Air Force Base. This administrative error ended up costing me $20,000. All too actually just end up at the unit I had joined when I originally enlisted, but had not yet been stood up or fully funded. I will leave you here with that little incident for later. It is yet another example of our government's seemingly complete disregard for those that serve, and honoring your word. But in the end, not getting the $20,000 bonus allowed me to take a job in Iraq for $240,000. You would not believe all the stories I have heard about promises made by recruiters, which ended up completely screwing the soldier. And with that, I hope you enjoy my next chapter, "The 40-Year-Old Private."

3   The 40-Year-Old Private
PVT Bergy's First Duty Station - Almost

Following my successful completion of basic training and AIT, I returned to Tampa for in-processing to my new unit, but as is always the case, there was a catch. While enlisting in the Army, the recruiter wanted to place me in a new reserve unit over at McDill AFB. It was considered one of the best signal outfits in the U.S. Military, and had all the best toys. This unit was called The Joint Communications Support Element, Army Reserve Element, or JCSE-ARE. Unfortunately, the 4th JCS hadn't yet been stood up and didn't have full funding when I enlisted, so my recruiter placed me with the 810 Military Police as an administrative trick to get me into the system. I didn't understand it all, but it sounded like a good idea. My Army enlistment came with a $20,000 bonus also, which I was to receive half of when I got to my unit. Unfortunately, because I processed into the 810 MP, and then processed right back out to JCSE, I wouldn't get my $20,000 Army enlistment bonus. Personally, I thought the bonus was for simply enlisting in the Army? It is called an enlistment bonus after all, but the recruiter, whom I'm sure knew this would disqualified me from my bonus, left that part out. It wouldn't have mattered to me anyway, as I had not enlisted for the money. That said, it still would have been nice to have received the $20,000 I was promised when enlisting. Looking back at it now, I am a bit concerned some of the recruiters might use this to get people to enlist that needed the money, then screw them out of it on an administrative technicality. If there is one thing I learned very quickly in the military, is not to trust anyone that works for the government. I was disappointed at the time, as $20,000 would have helped my family tremendously. I had spent over 30 weeks at basic training and AIT, all while living on the pay grade of a PV2. It didn't take long to really start biting into our family savings. It doesn't seem right to justify promising to pay someone $20,000, and then tell them, "sorry, didn't you read line 27 on page 125 of the enlistment contract you signed?" I don't remember the actual pages, but it was a lot. Even if it had said funding was only from the 810MP, which nobody ever actually showed me, I would have never thought that I would not get it because I transferred to JCSE. But now JCSE was fully funded and the first few people had started coming onboard. Also, as you will see a little bit later, it all worked out for the best anyway.

PVT Bergy's Second, First Duty Station

When I showed up at JCSE for my first weekend, there were only about 10 members. JCSE was a very technically advanced unit, using some of the most state of the art satellite and radio communications on the planet. JCSE consisted of four separate divisions, which I was told had an annual budget somewhere north of $300 million, but cannot confirm. There really wasn't but a few hundred members in all JCSE, and getting smaller, not larger.

Although enlistment was at an all-time low, and recruiters struggled to meet quota's, I was told Bill Clinton's attrition plan was still in effect, further reducing our troop levels, forcing our best and brightest that have served for 15-20 years into early retirement. I cringed when I found out that many of the soldiers that were soon to be joining us were still at AIT. This all sounds like a great plan, doesn't it? Nearly all the enlisted soldiers in JCSE held the rank of sergeant or above, and I was still just a PV2 when I arrived. I remembered from AIT one of the most common statements the teachers would make when you asked them a question they didn't know, was, "they will teach you that when you get to your unit." Unfortunately, just a few people in the JCSE-ARE had any actual working background in information technology, so PV2 Bergy came in useful in helping to stand up this new unit. Later, as new members of our reserve unit started arriving, we had some talented people come on board. Soon after that we started to put together the initial training materials and SOP's for deployment of our Small, Command and Control Satellite over IP (SC2IP) communication package.

Although I quickly advanced to the rank of PFC with the passing of my first JCSE physical fitness test, there were only a couple of us privates, and they were mostly much younger. Politics got involved here, and although my knowledge of IT networks and infrastructure was above average to most of the soldiers coming in with higher rank, many in my chain of command didn't want a PFC instructing a large group of commissioned and non-commissioned officers. I found that a bit odd, thinking why you wouldn't want the people with the most experience to teach their tacit knowledge to those with less experience – irrespective of their rank, how fast they could run or how many sit-ups they could do in two minutes. Nonetheless, I really enjoyed being a part of standing up this new, high speed signal command reserve element whose main client was CENTCOM, and considered as the "Tip of the Spear" in the war on terror. I was on the front line of the front lines, and it was a humbling experience. We had the best toys, technologically speaking, and for me it was like being in nerd heaven. Another thing I could see very quickly was that much like Fort Benning was learning how to adapt to the new enlistment age policies, so was JCSE. Now that 40-year-old men with no prior military experience were enlisting, it was creating a whole new dynamic for many commands. For one, I was a private that was twice the age of many of my superiors. I constantly found myself struggling to understand working for the U.S. government as well. Coming from the private sector, where, although we don't generally have to kill people and blow stuff up, the tech was the same. In the private sector, we were required to perform with much greater efficiency, pride in workmanship and responsibility. This working environment in the Army where physical endurance was more important than intellectual prowess was really something I was struggling with, both physically and mentally. Such priorities on a soldier's physical fitness has been engrained into the fabric of our military for centuries. Throughout most of our military's existence, brawn and a bigger boom was our military's primary force multiplier. Today, in the age of cyber warfare, social media and our dependence on global e-commerce, the war on terror is not limited to the battlefield. I fail to see how having a lower proficiency in push-ups, or my lower rank having enlisted at a much older age, should be a determining factor in the level of respect and responsibilities I am given by my colleagues. Physical endurance will always play a critical role in the military, but the value of someone with experience and knowledge as a subject matter expert in information technology could become a powerful force multiplier, if our military and government leaders really supported it.

No Help Wanted for Reserve Soldiers

Returning home to Tampa, and unemployed, having lost my job because of joining the Army in the first place, quickly brought my basic training and AIT graduation celebration to an abrupt end. I picked up some additional active duty time with standing up our new reserve unit, and when JCSE couldn't provide the hours, I worked doing contract IT support and installations for the public sector. This was tier one stuff, like installing point of sale systems in retail stores. The available work was temporary, and made maintaining our families existing home mortgage and other non-discretionary expenses nearly impossible. Yes, it is financially difficult when deployed on active duty orders with the rank of PFC, but it would have made a huge difference to have come home and had my job, or my $20,000 enlistment bonus waiting for me. I hope if anyone ever actually reads this book, they will remember how much our military and their families depend on their employers to be there for them when they return. Yes, it's a little harder to employ someone that can be deployed on orders in a moment's notice. It is harder on everyone, the employer, soldier, and their families, than it is to hire someone not in the reserves. But our reserve soldiers are a critical part of our nation's defense, and employers need to step up and do the right thing.

My wife worked in a salon doing hair as much as she could when I was on orders at McDill, and in Afghanistan, while still making time as a mother to care for our very young children. Our church and many in our community came together and helped, which was just amazing to me. Things had begun to get tough financially, but our family was doing fine, and I continued standing up our reserve unit and preparing for its first deployment. I had volunteered to go out on our units first deployment, and had been working and training for nearly a year. We were ready for our deployment to Afghanistan, and then, I get the news.... Honey, I think I'm pregnant. I had a beautiful and caring wife, Lara, which I was absolutely in love with for more than 15 years before we even had our first date. Together, we already had produced two beautiful daughters named Mia and Sarah, whom were at that time around six and four years old respectively. There was not a lot of planning that had gone into this addition to our family, and conception likely would be traced back to a very short time following my return from 30 plus weeks away from my wife while at AIT. When we went for the first ultra-sound, we were informed of a second surprise, my wife was pregnant with twins. There are few things in life that provide a greater high, and conversely, a greater low, at the exact same time. I was absolutely thrilled with the thought of another child, or two. But I was also concerned with an ever-thinning budget on the salary of a PFC, and I was preparing for our units first deployment to Afghanistan. When the ultra-sound technician tells you its twins, the math is simple, just double every known expense by two.

The stress of being deployed, along with the financial impact and the thought of now leaving my wife alone to care for four children, not two, was high, but I tried not to let it show. The news of the twins did significantly impact the dynamic of our family, and by extension, my mission. I didn't understand it at the time, but it would seem my commanding officer, LTC Dubrill, did. I didn't like what he had to say much at all, but he was correct, and yes, I can be a real idiot at times (spoiler alert). He told me that I was going to be pulled from the first deployment of JCSE-ARE, and go out on the second mission - after my sons were born.

I cannot honestly tell you what was going through my mind wanting to still deploy out with my team on the first mission. I can tell you I had put a lot of time and effort into training for the mission. My team was one of the best, if not the best in all JCSE. I love my family and I love my children with all my heart, but in my mind, I felt like I was being treated differently, as other soldiers much younger are literally deployed overseas when their children were born. Would this offer had been extended to someone 25 years old that was just married and had a child on the way? No, in most every case I have heard of or seen, the soldier would have deployed as planned.

It is about now you're thinking I want it both ways. You're thinking I want the military to be more understanding of issues as they relate to older recruits new to the military. On the other hand, you have heard me complain about how in basic training I was not allowed to do many of the things younger recruits are asked to do, like being a squad leader. During basic training, I really wanted my drill sergeant to pick me as a squad leader during at least one of our training missions, and I felt left out when I was not. When I asked why I was not being chosen, the drill sergeant told me that I already knew about leadership, and he wanted to use the time he was given at basic training to work with some of the younger recruits that didn't. They never expected this to bother me, but it did. I felt it was necessary to prove myself, maybe even greater to me than most any of the younger guys that would avoid taking leadership positions. By this time, you're starting to see how this new age dynamic in the military is getting a little more complicated than most would have expected. Most 40-year-old men with no prior military will not simply skate through the physical requirements of basic training. It takes every ounce of their being, both physically and mentally, and you will never maintain a strong success rate with older recruits if you don't address both issues. I think this is a healthy conversation to have, and may help to better understand my thinking when I was told I would not be deploying out with my team on our reserve units first mission. Not having a job when I got home from basic made the decision even more difficult, as I would have earned more being deployed to a combat zone, and now I was going to have two more mouths to feed. Thanks again Dr. Klein! I am starting to think you may have been right, and that this enlisting in the Army thing was a bad idea. Although, I am guessing you were basing that thought on the fact you knew I wasn't going to have a job when I returned at that time. Everything would have been much easier had I come home to my old job, trained on weekends with my unit, raised my children and deployed to Afghanistan with my unit to defend our country.

My First Deployment to Afghanistan

Following the birth of my twin sons back in January 2007, I continued to prepare for my upcoming deployment, and my next PT test. Hopefully I would pass the test and make the rank of Specialist, but the Army PT test was something I had become to dread. Such a tremendous emphasis was placed on this test and our daily exercise. Zero if any recognition was being placed on what I was doing for our unit in IT. Here is one example. What I did for JCSE and the Army Signal Support was to setup communications for commanders in what is called a TOC, and at the squad level as well so our commanders can have a clear operational picture of what is happening on the ground. JCSE had decided to make a little competition out of setting up our SC2IP (Small Command and Control over IP) package. This SC2IP was amazing, and although I was not with JCSE at the time, I understand it was setup during Hurricane Katrina in New Orleans to provide communications for state officials and emergency responders.

The SC2IP (pronounced "Skip") package consist of mostly all common-off-the-shelf (COTS) products, such as Cisco Phones, Laptops, and Windows Servers. All are installed in portable, rack mounted Tough Boxes – freaking very cool! A SWE-DISH suitcase satellite system that was largely automatic was used for connecting the SC2IP network from anywhere on the planet. Just put a few pieces of the dish together and enter the name of the satellite you want to use. It would automatically search the sky and lock onto the satellite with usually very little effort. I was still struggling with my PT scores and the daily exercise routine we had, but when it came to the SC2IP, our team was setting JCSE records for the time it would take to deploy the SC2IP. I don't want to reveal exactly how fast it takes, but in one competition we had with a group of special ops guys out of the 82nd Airborne that came to train with us one weekend, we literally blew their time out of the water by several minutes. So, tell me, if you were deployed overseas in combat, and your position was under attack and you needed communications with your command to call in support, would you rather have the guy next to you be the fastest runner, or the fastest at getting communications back on-line? The correct answer to that would of course be both. Not necessarily one or the other, but both. Would it be nice to have an IT guy that can also do 200 consecutive push-ups, of course. This scenario is exceptionally rare, though, especially in the military. I apologize, but compare the average IQ of a team of football players to the average IQ of a team of mathematicians, or a champion chess team, and I make my point. The trainers and most proficient in our highly technical communications unit were on average not the fastest or the strongest physically. The best IT guy in the 4th JCS smoked a pack of cigarettes a day, but still ran faster than me.

It was just a few weeks out from my deployment, and being pretty much the only PFC in our unit, my commander had my Spec 4 (Specialist) paperwork signed and ready to go. That is, just as soon as I pass my next physical fitness test. I had been training hard, but to be honest, I was struggling with the limitations of my now 42-year-old body balancing both work and now twin sons. I had essentially been pushed too hard, and too fast in the early stages of my training. I had struggled with injuries to my feet during basic training. I met the minimum requirements in both push-ups and sit-ups, but in my final PT test before my deployment, I came up 3 seconds short on my run time. The guy taking the time told me not to worry, and that he would show me as having passed. I heard this was common among some of the older officers and senior enlisted, but was not acceptable to me. I declined his offer because I could not wear a rank I didn't earn. The paperwork was already signed, and I had all but been officially promoted. The PT test had been a mere formality for everyone in my command but me. I really sort of regret my decision now not to just take the 3 seconds of time I was offered, but I am pretty sure even with such regrets today, that I would do it the same way again.

By this time, it was becoming clear to me that the physical requirements of the military were taking a toll, and I was not sure how much longer I would be able to last. Although many considered me one of the most proficient in my field of expertise at JCSE, the Army didn't really care. I was deploying to Afghanistan as a PFC, and not a specialist, which would have come with greater salary and the simple fact you are no longer a 42-year-old private. In most cases, an older person with the rank of a private is someone that at one point had a higher rank, but did something jacked-up and was busted down in his or her rank. I frequently had to explain the fact I was one of the first 40-year old's to complete basic training, so people wouldn't just assume I was a 42 year old screw up. This was an issue that really started to suck for me personally. I was one of the best in JCSE at what I did, but was stuck at the rank normally associated with a screw-up. I know our military can't consist of a bunch of fat old people sitting around smoking cigarettes and drinking coffee. I get that, and this is not the point I was trying to argue. By any standard I was in the best shape of my life, and I owed that to my Army training. But what needs to happen is that the physical requirements set forth by the military in certain specialty fields, need to become based on a soldiers MOS (military occupational specialty), and not solely on the PT test in a one size fits all fashion. Yes, the time requirements go down as you get older. When I turned 42, my minimum time went from 18:18 to 18:40, and that is great. What they need to do is that for doctors and many of those in the IT security fields, these tests should not be meant to break someone, but rather to make them better.

So, I am preparing to deploy, and we have a whole list of stuff you need to have done. Medical, dental, insurance paperwork, DoD passport, your orders. The list is pretty long so I will stop there, but the one item I specifically included was my orders, and you will see why when I discuss what happened later in my deployment. The Army, I found out rather quickly, is not the best when it comes to administrative tasking. Oddly enough I went on later in my career (and in this book), to develop better, more effective, and efficient ways for the Army to handle administrative tasks like processing orders. Not so surprising will you find that didn't end very well due to the other problem the Army has, and that is the stupidity of most government employees. But let's not get ahead of ourselves and get back to my first deployment to Afghanistan.

It's now just days before we are scheduled to deploy to Afghanistan. I have all of my medical, dental and such ready, but someone forgot to submit a request for our orders, and our passports. Even the adjudication of my Top-Secret / SCI clearance came down to the last minute. Seriously, nobody could make this stuff up. The passports were somehow expedited at the last minute through official channels, and our orders came through literally just hours before we were set to fly out. Imagine how successful a private company would be if it was that disorganized. It was my first trip abroad, and I was heading off to a war zone with the other 3 guys on my team, and a Top-Secret suitcase that contained, well, Top-Secret stuff. I deployed with another IT guy and two air conditioning repairmen to a baking hot desert in the middle east. That was smart, if you ask me. We had to stop and change flights in Greece. We were not allowed to travel in uniform, and I remember running into this young Greek security guard at the Airport who spoke or read no English at all. I had an official U.S. government DoD passport, official currier card and letter stating the contents of the case I was carrying was protected under diplomatic immunity, and that nobody can search it, scan it or even touch it. When I handed the guard my U.S. Diplomatic passport and official papers stating that, he showed it to the even younger colleague working next to him. They discussed something in Greek for a few moments, (I couldn't understand as it was all Greek to me. Ha ha) then looked at me with shrugged shoulders and said with an almost Chief Inspector Jacques Clouseau accent, "I hope it's not a bomb," and let me pass with my Top-Secret case unmolested. I don't know which was more concerning, his complete disregard of a potential alternate answer to the bomb question he just asked, or the fact I could have handed him a copy of an IRS W2 form and he wouldn't have known the difference, as neither of them could read English.

Welcome to Kandahar

It took a long time to finally arrive in Afghanistan. We arrived at an airport terminal in Kandahar known as the TLS terminal facility, which was short for "Taliban's Last Stand" at Kandahar Air Force Base (KAF). This was the location of the last fight of the original Taliban leadership, and now sports a huge hole in its roof from a JDAM missile. A flag was placed inside the building and goes out through the JDAM hole in the roof. Soldiers stationed there can have their personal flags raised above the TLS building, and given a certificate showing that it was flown there. I had a flag flown for my church, and presented it to them when I returned. I later purchased a beautiful flag pole for them as well. I don't want to speak much about my church, its pastor, and the role it played in my life during this 10-year story. It is likely not what you would have expected, I for one sure didn't expect it.

After we arrived and got settled in, we got our mission briefing and had some time to take a tour of KAF. The Canadians were stationed there, and in typical Canadian fashion had built an outdoor hockey rink and a Tim Horton's Coffee shop in the center of the base. Canadian's sure love their Timmy's and hockey. American troops got The Green Bean, AKA, "The Bean", which was the U.S. military's version of Starbucks.

 There was a boardwalk area with a TGI Friday's, although the prices were too high for a PFC. Shortly after I got there, a few generals felt our troops might get too soft if they had to many nice things, like real food and a friendly atmosphere from a place that reminded them of home, so they ended up closing the TGI Friday's just as we were leaving. There were many businesses like that from the states overseas, and most of us thought it was good for morale to have some of the comforts of home once and a while. I would be one of those people that believe we should do everything we can to provide our troops with that "touch of home." This "touch of home" is something I personally have been involved with through a veteran based non-profit I founded with some friends, but that is for later in this story. For now, let's continue with my time in Kandahar.

The Fusion Cell

When I walked into my "office," known as the Kandahar Fusion Cell, on the first day, I was really impressed with the technology and hardware. It was like something right out of, and even beyond, the TV show '24,' with Kieffer Sutherland. Giant flat screen monitors hooked up to the latest technology, most, if not all of the "toys" we got to play with for conducting ISR (Intelligence, Surveillance and Reconnaissance) is way to classified to discuss. The analogy using the show 24 was not by accident, as everyone in the "fusion cell," would watch the 24 series on the bootleg DVD's we bought right on base. They would sell them right in front of the PX and other places, but the command never said a thing. It bothered me that our command allowed the sale and distribution of illegal movies, most of which were illegal copies from China. I am positive the Chinese were putting malware on the DVD's knowing that U.S. military is using them. If they didn't exploit such an obvious vulnerability, then they are the biggest idiots on the planet.

I didn't make many friends with this position, and in fact as the Information Assurance Security Officer for our unit, it was my job to inform my command. Soldiers were literally putting these illegal DVD's into government computers classified as TOP-SECRET – IN THE FUSION CELL!!! Once again, I was the one that was the asshole for pointing out this obvious security threat. You have no idea the trouble this caused me. My commanders looked at me like a nark, and just trying to cause trouble, largely because it was 2007 and most in our command didn't understand IT security. Nobody wanted to watch movies and TV programs on our off hours more than me, but I couldn't just sit by and watch people do such stupid things. My warnings went unheeded, and people kept on with business as usual in complete violation of DoD regulations, and just violating common sense. Think about it, if you purchase and watch an illegally pirated DVD with the big FBI warning shown at the beginning stating you are in violation of numerous federal and international laws even just watching it, you could technically lose your clearance. But you will find, just as I did in a very short period of time, that people enforce the rules they like, and ignore the rules they don't. Hillary Clinton and her private email server come to mind here. This rule, however, from an IT security perspective, is not a rule that should have been allowed to be ignored or overlooked. Generals were perfectly fine with allowing DVD's purchased from Afghan men working on base selling rugs, DVD's, and other stuff, who could easily have ties to the Taliban, but what do they focus on, taking away our TGI Friday's? I am writing this book as a non-fiction autobiography, not a fictional fantasy. But even some of the best fiction writers could not make stuff up that is this ridiculous. Years later, and I will give you just a small bit about the veteran based non-profit I founded for context now, and save the rest for later in the story. But years later I came up with a way through a non-profit to provide legal, licensed, video on demand services to our men and women overseas. Our troops were still purchasing illegal DVD's all around the world anywhere they were stationed. Those that weren't purchasing the discs, were downloading their movies online using illegal torrents. They would hide who they are (or think they're hiding) by using these free DNS and VPN proxy servers online, but the problem with that was many of those companies are either owned by the Chinese, or by who knows where? The very nature of these types of internet services is based on anonymity, and most efforts to understand where your data is being routed will be fruitless, but the data you think is encrypted or private, can be potentially be seen by the administrators and owners of these clandestine servers. Most of our troops deployed overseas don't just use these services for downloading illegal videos, and many DNS Proxy services require software to be installed locally on your computer. I have written blog posts and whitepapers warning soldiers and our government officials of what is potentially one of the greatest national security vulnerabilities in our lifetime. You will have to wait for the chapter about my veterans based non-profit to find out what happens and how it ends, but yes, it ends just like you probably expected if you have read this far into my book. I take that back, as there is no way in hell anyone would have expected this level of government corruption, incompetence, and stupidity as it relates to my veterans based non-profit I discuss later in my book.

For all the technology at our disposal in the Fusion Cell, the old adage of "garbage in, garbage out" still applied. You can collect all the data in the world, and pinpoint a missile to within a few meters of a cell phone from a thousand miles away, but whenever I listen to our leaders in Washington praising the capabilities of drones, I wonder if they have any idea of what they are talking about. It's politically dangerous to suggest putting boots on the ground, or putting our troops in harm's way, so drones are a seemingly political safe way of looking like you are doing something. But war is inherently bloody, deadly, and very messy. We like to think we take every possible measure to reduce collateral damage, and the truth is, compared to wars of the past, we do. Technology has eliminated the need of mass aerial bombings over populated cities, allowing us pin-point accuracy of specific targets. Our job in the Fusion Cell was to bring together all of our partner countries most elite units under the single command of ISAF forces, (affectionately known to most U.S. troops as "I Suck At Fighting"). When I first arrived in Kandahar, the U.S. flag was flown at KAF, and the U.S. essentially ran things. Around the time I was leaving, the ISAF flag had replaced the U.S. flag, and all operations at that time fell under the command of ISAF. As you can imagine, this was the cause of a great deal of problems when it came to authorizing air strikes and other missions.

The dissemination process for the intelligence we collected was very thorough. But even the best possible decisions are nearly always going to be based on the collection and dissemination of multiple sources of ISR (Intelligence, Surveillance, and Reconnaissance). Sometimes, no matter how hard you try, you are just going to get it wrong. Sadly, this is nothing new or specific I am referring to, but incidents involving drones are widely reported in the media. These media reports most often are reported days after something happens. I think based on my personal experience and knowledge, it is important that people understand this main point. With all the lives that are saved by these new technologies, they are not perfect, and we need to use it not as our first resort, but as a last resort. Drones should only be used when placing our soldiers on the ground is impossible. Even then, I am not sure. What I am sure about is that politics needs to stay far from the battlefield, but never does.

Our victories in Afghanistan were sweet, and when we made a mistake at the office, it usually meant a lot of pain for a lot of people. That's just what war is, and you must accept this is going to happen before you start, or don't start it in the first place. But imagine, as an example, what you would do if one day at the office, a day that started just like many others, ended with a mistake that left over a hundred women and children in small, burning pieces and parts scattered about a large field, after an A10 Warthog hit them with several 200 – 500-pound guided bombs? Would you maybe start to question the limitations of these new technologies? Would you replay over and over the video images etched in your mind of the bodies of those children for the rest of your life? Would you feel responsible, even if you didn't pull the trigger, so to speak? A life at war is not for the weak of heart, I can tell you that. I can also tell you that the work we were doing in advancing the common operational picture on the battlefield will someday eliminate mistakes that were made in the past. At least this is what I tell myself to help me sleep at night. I tell you one thing for sure, I am so grateful that my children won't ever have to go through what the children and their mothers in Afghanistan have had to go through. My children won't live this kind of life because what we were doing over there by taking this fight to them, makes it very hard for them to bring the fight to my family's door. For that, I am exceptionally proud to have been involved in such a critical part of the war on terror. Irrespective to the argument of how it began and if we should have gone there in the first place. We were there now, and American's need to stand up and protect our homeland from a very large and organized group of religious nutjobs that see our freedoms as an affront to their way of life, and their faith.

Kandahar Air Base was really an amazing place. It was stood up in a very short period of time, and so much credit needs to go out to the Seabee's. I think they could build a bridge out of match sticks if they had enough of them. Most of waste and corruption came from the foreign contractors, and I don't mean just the U.S. contracts. When we first arrived at our quarters in KAF, there was a huge concrete slab, seemingly the size of a football field. The concrete was poured, well; poorly to say the least. The building that was supposed to have been built there was stopped prior to it even being started due to the fact the local Afghan company hired to build it ran off with the millions of dollars in deposit money. This also happened to the building I was working in while I was in Iraq as well, which I will tell you about later, but not on this scale. The building was supposed to be built to house equipment for a troop "surge" that never happened. By the time they got around to building the pre-fabricated aluminum structure, costing 100's of millions of dollars, they didn't need it anymore. It was a massive building that was nearly finished just as I was leaving, and to my knowledge, was never even going to be used for anything more than

maybe storing a few trucks. Again, this was the size of a football field, but was pretty much used as a common, backyard tool shed.

The shower tent was an interesting story and a good example of the dysfunction found in a war zone. The first few days after we arrived we could take a warm shower, which you wouldn't think would be that big of a deal when it is 130 degrees outside during the day. However, when the generator that runs the hot water heater breaks, you get just cold water from this huge tank outside. I think because it is freezing cold at night? For 2 weeks, I asked what the problem was with the showers, and for 2 weeks they said the generator was broken and parts were on their way. After about 3 weeks we discovered the generator was simply out of gas, and that the refueling truck forgot to fill it up. Stupid, silly things like that can really make a big difference in your day. You don't expect the comforts of home when you deploy to a war zone, but when incompetence is the factor for a hundred-people screaming every morning from when the cold water hits their private part, you really want to throttle the jacked-up solder that failed to do his assigned mission.

Our sleeping quarters was a large tent shared by a dozen or so men. The Wi-Fi access we had was extremely expensive, and they limited the bandwidth to a crawl, making video chats with the family back home pretty much impossible once we were off work. There was a USO tent close to us that had some internet and a TV, but it was even slower. When I think of what our government could have done to provide a good way for our troops deployed overseas to stay connected to their families, friends and yes, TV shows, with just the money that was wasted on that one building I talked about earlier, I am just saddened to my core.

My time in Kandahar was easy for sure compared to those that went outside the gate. I had volunteered on several occasions to leave the base on missions to provide ground support, but was never allowed. Apparently, someone thought that what we were providing to the command was too important to risk sending us out. The base was very secure, and although there were incidents at other locations where the Taliban had infiltrated some bases and blew themselves up, or grabbed a soldier's weapon and started shooting people, this never happened on KAF while I was deployed there. That said, the thought of this happening was always close in your mind. We had alarms quite often that would flail loudly and repeat the words "incoming, incoming, incoming", warning us of potential mortars and such, but nothing serious ever happened until the day we left when the enemy… Nope, you will have to wait for the next chapter I call "The Poo Pond."

The Poo Pond

Depending on the direction of the wind, you cannot visit KAF and not be immediately aware of its presence. It is a perfectly round "pond" that is several acres in size, and separated into 4 equal parts. There are times during the day, when the wind is just right, during the blistering heat of the summer in KAF, and the temperature exceeds something like 130 Fahrenheit, that going into a portable outhouse, smells better than it does outside. That is not a joke, and that outhouse has not just been emptied recently. It is truly overwhelming at

ISAF.NATO.INT

times, and at others, it provided an escape from the hustle and bustle of the main part of the base, to a view of a "lake"?

There was a perimeter road that surrounded the shit pond. On one side of the road was the pond, and on the other, a mine field. If the incoming alarm sounded and you were out on that road, I am not sure if I would seek cover down the bank of the pond, or in the mine field, but had already planned in that event to use the mine field. If you remember a few chapters back, I deployed to Kandahar having failed my PT test by 3 seconds. I needed to keep training while in Kandahar so that when I returned, I would be able to make my run time. You can fail your PT test a few times in the Army and it mostly effects only your promotions. But if you continue to fail, you will be kicked out of the Army, no matter how good you are at your job.

I worked out at the gym, but I also could eat really, really well. I believe at the time in Kandahar the DFAC, which is where you eat, was being run by KBR. I know for sure in Iraq KBR held the contract for Camp Victory, and oh my God... The steak and lobster Friday's story is for the next chapter. In Kandahar, it was nothing to sneeze at. Breakfast, lunch, and dinner was all you can eat, and there were no drill sergeants lurking around the corner to bust you for that glass of milk, or cup of coffee. Our shift was 12 hours on and 12 hours off, which didn't leave much time before you crashed for the night to get stuff done and work out. Although I had quit smoking for almost 7 years prior to my enlisting in the Army, after completing basic training and going to AIT, I started smoking again. Everyone did it and there was a lot of boredom there. I still kick myself to this day for starting to smoke again, and it didn't help while at a very high altitude in Kandahar that summer with my two-mile run training. Not only was Kandahar ridiculously hot, it was also at a very high altitude, which makes running even more difficult, and my run time became even worse. We had a nice gym for weights, and I have never had any trouble with my push-ups or sit-ups since passing basic training, but my run time was my weakness. So, I began running outside, and the path to judge our 2-mile distance takes you a few times all the way around the poo pond. Could this PT issue be any more difficult? Seriously. I pushed myself hard, and in the first few weeks at KAF I herniate a disc in my back unloading a pallet of Gatorade. Not really a combat wound you would hold up next to a Purple Heart recipient, but nonetheless very painful and impacted my training a lot. I kept it up, and about 3 months into my deployment in Kandahar I had another PT test to see where my progress was, and I had gotten worse. My best time was going as much as a minute or more over the required time for a man of my age. I can list all the usual excuses, such as altitude, bad back, heat and such, and those are all pretty good excuses, but I also wasn't mentally pushing myself in the way that is necessary to maintain this level of fitness. I think a lot of that had to do with the mental state you get in a war zone. The day to day stress is much greater than a usual day at the office for most people back home.

I continued to excel in my work, developing tasking tools in SharePoint for administrative functions, as well as tactical applications that allowed our command to see a clearer and more real time COP, or Common Operational Picture of the battlefield. I got to help beta test software that provided our command with some serious next-gen COP. I cannot go into details, or even generalize the stuff we were working on, but it was providing our troops on the ground with more situational awareness than ever before. Sitting here writing this nearly 8 years later, I cannot even begin to imagine where they have taken the initial work we were doing since then.

I loved being a soldier. I loved what we were doing in Afghanistan. I went there to punish the Taliban and those that attacked us on September 11th. To that end, I did get those that died on 9/11 some serious payback! Unfortunately, when I arrived, I found there was a different story that I had never heard about in the news. Most people find this quite shocking, but the Taliban had nothing to do with September 11th. Even more shocking is what would you think if I told you the Taliban leadership hated and feared Bin Laden even more than we did? Now, before you think I am some Taliban sympathizer, I am not. The Taliban are the filth of the earth. I have never seen a more shameful, backwards, bullshit culture in my life. Here's an example of how utterly messed up these people are. The Koran forbids a man from having sex with his wife unless they are trying to conceive a child. Some Afghanistan guy decided to interpret this as meaning it is ok to sleep with your male neighbor, or to have sex with a donkey. They coined this day of the week as "man love Thursday." This is not a joke, and I am not making this up. I have witnessed this watching aerial video from drones and lookout towers. Most of these people are literally just shit bags. But that said, you don't kill people because they want to bang other dudes and donkeys on Thursday, because Allah didn't say you couldn't do it. It just pretty much means I am not going to make plans to summer there.

Bin Laden had a beautiful, walled compound in Kabul and was initially living there under the protection of the Taliban. But then something happened, and the Taliban leadership started to feel threatened by Bin Laden, and he was exiled to the mountainous regions along the Pakistan border. By the time September 11th happened, Bin Laden wasn't under the protection of the Taliban. Sure, there were factions within the Taliban that were loyal to Bin Laden, which is why the Taliban leadership became worried and exiled him. Call it self-preservation, but don't confuse who we were fighting in Afghanistan as the same people responsible for 9/11 like I did for a long time.

Look at it like this, the U.S. military has a lot of white supremacists within its ranks, but that doesn't mean everyone in the military is a member of the KKK, or even espouse to their way of thinking. This doesn't make me want to kill them any less after what I saw when our troops would come back to base all blown to pieces. This isn't why we went in there in the first place, and I think that is important to acknowledge. Even if they weren't our enemies before, they, and others like Al Qaida in Iraq, and ISIS, are now, and they need to be stopped using our military forces. We need to bring the fight to them, before they bring the fight to our local malls and government buildings. It was not going to be an easy fight, and like with all wars there are going to be both victory, and mistakes.

As I mentioned at the end of the last chapter, there were really no incidents on base the entire time I was there, until the day I left. On the edge of the poo pond stood the KBR laundry facility. Wow, what a stunning waterfront view they had there. Anyway, on the day I was flying out, the enemy let loose with the most devastating and demoralizing mortar attacks yet. A single mortar round landed about 50 or so meters behind the KBR laundry facility, right into the shit pond. This released approximately a 300-meter spray of shit everywhere, and undoubtedly added a new, fresh scent too the uniforms waiting to be picked up.

I look at the situation in Iraq and Afghanistan in much the same way I look at the poo pond. You never really wanted it, and the wind is constantly changing so you never really know when the smell of poo is going to hit you, but you're sure glad you had someplace to put it when it hits the fan.

"Short Time"

I was just 30 or so days out from returning home, which was affectionately known as "short time" in the military. I got a call from my 1st Lieutenant that he needed to speak with me. When I arrived in his office he asked me to sit down and told me there was a small problem. I immediately thought the worst, like something happened to my wife or my children. One of my greatest stresses while deployed is with my family. I have 4 children, a wife, and a mortgage, all of which have been without me for a long time, and the salary of a PFC, even while deployed, made paying bills a constant struggle. What happened next absolutely took me by surprise, and I must say total disappointment in my command.

The 1st LT, which I won't mention his name because he is so worthless, tells me that there was a problem with my orders, and that I was not going to get paid for the last month I was deployed in Afghanistan. He said "but don't worry, you probably will still get paid (probably?) But in the meantime, here is a phone number that you can call to get a low interest loan to help you and your family get by until you are back home." I swear to God, hand on a stack of bibles I could not make this up, and in fact this entire incident is on record. I calmly asked if that was all, then that I would like to be excused. I walked out the door and almost started to cry – which is not authorized in a war zone, but happens more than you might think. It is a lot on a man, a father, to leave his family to go to war and fight for his country, and this was something I knew when I volunteered. But I always felt that no matter what you see on a day to day basis in a combat zone, your command and your country would be there for your family. I went back to my desk and decided to write my commander back home and see what was going on, if this could be true. It was not a letter a PFC writes his commanding officer, it was a man, writing to another man, asking what was going on? Well, remember a few chapters back and it was the day before we were scheduled to leave and our orders were not in yet. In rushing those orders, whom I was told was put together by the same, worthless butter bar that gave me the phone number to take out a loan, a mistake was made and I was only funded for 5 months, but my orders were for 6. This didn't happen to anyone else but me on the team, and to make matters worse, nobody would guarantee me in writing that I was even going to get back pay in 30 days. It's like I said before, this butter bar might be able to run fast in a PT test, which is really handy if you're Forrest freaking Gump, but it doesn't make you qualified to be in an administrative or leadership position. It just means you're a fast runner. Even thinking back to that moment now in writing this book I can't believe it happened to me.

So, after receiving an email from my JCSE command telling me to basically suck it up and deal with it, and not holding anyone responsible for this, I decided to take a walk down to the Inspector General's office on base in Kandahar. When I told the two IG captains what had happened, they both grabbed their head gear and said, "Come with us." We got into their SUV and they just flew across base to the office of our 1st LT. They essentially said to him that this PFC just told us this crazy story that cannot be true… Is it true? My 1st LT explained that yes, it was true, but we are working to try and correct it. The IG told him in no uncertain terms "that nobody on my base is going to be here, in a war zone on orders, and not be getting paid" He went on to say, "you know this private has a wife and children back home that are depending on his salary?" The IG then asked, "did you actually give him a phone number and recommend to this private he take out a low interest loan for a mistake that you made?" shaking his head in disgust. He told the 1st LT they had 2 days to fix the problem, or they needed to have me on a flight back to the states by the weeks end. To many, leaving KAF would have been a dream come true, but not to me. I had volunteered to come here, and we were doing some amazing stuff. I didn't want to leave yet. That said, my family could not afford a lapse in pay of 4 weeks or more, as we were living paycheck to paycheck. Even our church was helping and raised over $700.00 that they gave to my family. The support from my community back home was amazing, but the support from within my chain of command was at best, incompetent, and at worst, criminally negligent. And as you will soon discover, their incompetence soon turns to retaliation against me for reporting this to the Inspector General.

What would anyone do if something like this happened? Would you keep your mouth shut? Let your family go without food while you apply for a loan that puts your family further into debt? With no assurance that you were ever going to get paid for your last month in a war zone? People all the time question my actions, whether for reporting security incidents, abuse, fraud, or in this case, incompetence. The way I see it is that if I don't speak up and say something, then how is the problem ever going to get fixed, or better yet, be prevented in the future from happening to someone else. There were four people that deployed with me to Afghanistan, that's four orders that needed to be put through the system and properly funded. People do this for hundreds of troops at a time without so much as a single issue, so should this 1st LT and my commander get a pass for such a huge mistake, or should there be what we call in the Army's After Action Report (AAR), a "Lessons Learned" moment?

I had the honor, and the distinct privilege to have served my country in a time of war at The Fusion Cell. It's the "tip of the spear" for all southern Afghanistan command and control operations for CENTCOM and the war on terror.

In just two years' time, I had gone from a failed candidate for Supervisor of Elections in Pasco County, Florida, to providing critical, "tip of the spear" mission support for 4-star generals and coalition forces in Afghanistan. I was granted one of the highest-level clearances you can obtain in the department of defense. How I survived basic training at 40, let alone the height to which I could advance is still beyond my wildest imagination. I really had done a lot of good, and had proven a lot of people wrong that thought I would never make past basic training (myself included). But now, faced with the retaliation from my command for going to the Inspector General and filing a complaint, I am forced to fight yet another battle.

My command was unable to get funding that would keep me in Afghanistan for the remaining few weeks of my deployment, and I was ordered to ship home, ahead of my team and alone. Whether intentional retaliation or not, the next few months would prove to be the most difficult yet. My flight back was apparently on such short notice that my itinerary landed me somewhere in Turkey, where I was left stranded in a 100-man transient tent for about a week or so. What a nightmare that was, although I did make a new Air Force friend, Anthony, for whom I remain friends with to this day through Facebook and such. Other than that, I was really feeling quite abandoned by my command, and very much missing my family. I finally made it back to Tampa, and when I arrived at the airport in uniform and stepped off the plane, I was greeted by my wife and children in what was likely the greatest and most memorable moments in my entire life. It is just like what you see in the

YouTube video's when a soldier returns home to his family. I just broke down in tears, crying, hugging, and holding my children and wife for the first time in nearly 6 months. It is a moment so emotional, I am having a hard time even typing it now for the book. It is like having every single emotion that a person can have being triggered all at the same time. For that moment, all of the stress from the last six months disappeared. But it wasn't long before I was to face the consequences for going outside of my chain of command with my complaint to the IG, and my command was not shy about letting me know it.

Although I had flown out a few weeks ahead of my team, I got back just a few days before them thanks to the wonderful people at JCSE responsible for my itinerary. I in-processed back into the 4th JCS just like everyone else did that returned from deployment to their reserve unit, but unlike everyone else, I was not allowed to leave my unit from 8am to 5pm. I remained on orders doing menial tasks at a non-deployed, PFC salary. When the 1st LT returned from Afghanistan, things got even worse, and the retaliation was constant. Everyone else from my team returned and were taken off their orders and went back to their regular jobs. I went to my command and asked why I was being treated differently, and they denied I was. Many things started happening, which I won't go into detail with now, but it was clear it was retaliation for the trouble I had caused in KAF over my pay being stopped. Finally, after discussing options with my wife, I went to the IG at MacDill AFB where I was stationed and told them about what had happened. I was not being able to leave like the others and get a job so I could properly support my family.

I had responded to a job listing with a private military contracting company named, Dynology. They had an opening in Iraq for a position I was qualified for, and I held the required Top-Secret clearance for as well. After filing this new retaliation complaint against my command, I was taken into the 4th JCS office with my command. I told them that forcing me to stay a month longer than anyone else doing bullshit work, not even training, was harming my family and my ability to provide for them, and felt it was in retaliation for what happened in Afghanistan. I told them I had a job opportunity with a company in Iraq that would provide enough money to get my family out of the red and make us financially whole, but couldn't accept the job because I was still on orders, and nobody could give me a reason. That is when they offered me a deal. They said drop the IG complaint, and we will not only release you from orders, but we will release you from your remaining military service and place you into IRR (Individual Ready Reserve) with a full and honorable discharge. Now, if you remember back at the beginning of the book when I told you about the $20,000 signing bonus that I was supposed to have gotten, but didn't. Well, because I never got that signing bonus, and with the length of my combat deployment and time spent stateside on active duty orders, I had satisfactorily completed my required time in service. Had I received the $20k, I would have been committed to another full 4 years. There was simply no more fight left in me at this point, so I agreed to their conditions. I dropped the IG complaint filed in Afghanistan, which had been handed off to the IG at CENTCOM. I dropped the following retaliation complaint as well. With the emails I had from several people responsible for what happened to me in Afghanistan, this could have been a career buster for them all. It could have been a stain on their record for future promotions as well, and rightfully so. I called back Joel, from Dynology, setup a meeting and I was hired quick as that. I had entered the Army on 13 October 2005, and left the Army on 15 October 2007. Unbelievably, life was only just now starting to get interesting. I was going to Iraq, and my mission was good!

I wanted to take a moment once again to make very clear If you're hoping to read of some "Snowden" like leaking of Top-Secret information, you can stop reading now. You won't find it here. Both Snowden and I raised our hand and pledged an oath to not discuss what we did or saw when it pertains to classified information. I consider this man a traitor, and he should be punished in the most severe manner allowed by law for his crimes. There is nothing wrong with a man of Snowden's background and resume discussing with the IT community the importance of IT security and how to ensure your privacy. If these were all issues that were well documented publicly, he could have helped by educating people on the importance of things such as encryption, without ever releasing classified documents that put innocent people's lives in danger. There were even official reports in the early 2000's which related to Telecoms working with the government, so why not just become active and point out public facts to push change, rather than violating your oath? If someone was a drone pilot and witnessed countless lives lost due to inaccurate intelligence, and wants to make a difference without violating national security, that pilot can try to effect change by speaking out publicly as a citizen, using hundreds of news reports, and never speaking of specific missions he flew that led him to his beliefs and convictions. I won't discuss what I witnessed as a contractor in Iraq working as a system administrator and Information Assurance Security Officer for the 4th Psychological Operations Group if it is classified, but I will talk about the very deep concerns I have with the use of Interactive Internet Activities by governments and corporations around the world through manipulation of social media.

4   The Contractor - Bound for Baghdad

After another talk with my children about going away for a
while, and with the promise of a nice pool if they were good and
listened to their mother, everyone was good with daddy leaving
again. But this time I was going to Baghdad, Iraq, as a private
military contractor for 1 full year. As a contractor, I didn't have the
stress of PT tests, which was nice. With a salary and bonuses of
nearly $240,000 for my services for a year, well, money shouldn't be
an issue anymore either. I was thinking that I had essentially
removed the two biggest issues I had as a private deployed in
Afghanistan, so what could possibly go wrong, right?

I left Tampa behind and was now heading back to Fort
Benning, where the CONUS Relocation Center, or CRC was located.
The nostalgia was short lived though as I was immediately reminded
that I was back under the control of the government, only now it was
as a contractor. CRC was where civilians (and some military) would
go prior to deploying to a war zone. You had the same stupid tests,
some tactical training, and a lot of hurry up and wait. CRC was
supposed to take about 10 days or so, but again was an
administrative error that was discovered. A few days into CRC I
was told I would be required to leave. My contracting information
was not uploaded by my company correctly into the DoD's TASS
system. They wanted me to leave for 2 weeks and come back again

during the next cycle. The only thing I was missing to make it to Iraq was a CAC card, or a common access card, used by the military as your ID for base access, and to access DoD computer networks. Although I was forced to leave CRC prior to receiving my contractor CAC, my boss, Jim Jones, asked me if I still had my military ID, and I said yes. Dynology then booked me on the next commercial flight to Kuwait, and I was on my way to Iraq. Clearly, we cut some corners there that would come back to haunt me, as you will see in a later chapter when I return to Afghanistan. I will save that bit of fun later.

I arrived in Kuwait at an American military base, and had to go through military customs to enter Iraq. One of the necessary items for the customs pre-check was, you guessed it, my contractor CAC. Apparently, it is a big no-no to travel into country on a military CAC as a contractor. The initial response was that I had to return to the states and get my CAC at CRC in Fort Benning. Oh, snap! That's not good. I called my POC in Baghdad and explained to them the problem, then this AWESOME Colonel gets on the phone and starts yelling at the guy holding me up in customs, and the next thing you know I am on my flight to Baghdad. Landing in Baghdad at the airport in Camp Victory was a jaw dropping, stomach churning experience. Having lived in Tampa for years, I loved to visit Busch Gardens and ride all the roller coasters. This, however, was not a roller coaster ride, it was a spiraling death plunge, taking you from about 30,000 feet in the air, to the ground in a spiraling, corkscrew manner. I would call it a controlled crash, but there was little that felt controlled at any time. We landed, and I was met at the airport by the program manager, Russ Hampsey. I was exhausted and he drove me back to camp victory to get settled into my new temporary home, otherwise known as a transient tent. Having been to Afghanistan for 6 months and never seeing any action, I stashed my stuff and hopped into my top bunk to get some sleep. It was a long journey, and I had gotten no sleep the entire time in Kuwait due to the problem with my CAC. Within about an hour, I realized I was not in Afghanistan (or Kansas) anymore. I awoke to about 5 seconds of the loudspeaker saying "incoming, incoming, incoming", and boom…. boom…., boom. A total of 3 mortar rounds landed about 50 meters from our tent, and although protected by these giant steel reinforced concrete "T" walls, the wave from the blast knocked me out of my top bunk and onto the ground. I lay flat on the floor with my hands covering my head and proceeded to repeat the following "what the fuck am I doing here, what the fuck am I doing here, what the fuck am I doing here." And that, my friends, is how Baghdad welcomes its newest guests. Strange as it sounds, I stood my bunk back up, which had fallen against the one next to it, got back into bed, and slept like a baby the rest of the night.

Russ met me again the next morning and he took me on the usual "windshield" tour of Camp Victory, Camp Liberty and Stryker. The place was amazing. Aw-Faw Palace was in the center of Victory. It was Saddam Hussain's former palace, and it was magnificent. Not far from Aw-Faw was his son's, Uday and Qusay's palace. As I understand there was a room in there where unspeakable things were done to women by these two guys. The palace home of Saddam's two sons sat in the middle of a large lake, surrounded on all sides by water and just a single drive that extended from the main road out to the smaller palace. Although almost nobody at the time knew, it was where they had held Saddam during his trial. From the main road, you could see a huge hole in the roof from where a JDAM had hit its target perfectly. I found that to be a fitting place for Saddam to spend his final days. That said, as I will explain later after speaking with the Iraqi Special Forces people we were working with, many of the things we thought we knew about Saddam's Iraq, we not as we were led to believe. I find that when you are there, speaking with the people and not just listening to CNN or FOX, you become even less sure as to why we ever went there in the first place. As one example, so as not to have people tearing up my book and labeling me as a Saddam sympathizer, most people, myself included, were not aware that prior to our going into Iraq to remove Saddam, Iraq was the only country in the region where your children could attend both Christian and Catholic schools. In fact, many Iraqi fathers I met told me their children were going to a Christian school right there in Baghdad. That is until we went in, removed Saddam, and then allowed AQI (Al Qaida in Iraq) to move in and blew them all up in Saddam's absence. I bet you didn't know that, did you. Most people don't know we did find weapons of mass destruction in Iraq just shortly after we went in there. What, we didn't find any weapons of mass destruction! If we had, Bush would have been right back out on that "mission accomplished" ship telling the world he was right. Problem for Bush was that all the WMD we found, said "Made in America" on it, and were sold to Saddam by Donald Rumsfeld and company. So, the big press release never happened. But we found them!

In my first few weeks in Baghdad, mortar rounds were coming in daily. Things got a little better when I finally got moved from the transient tent to my new hooch. The hooch was a long trailer home that was divided into 2 or 3 sections. Each section was a room that held two people, or a single GS 14 and up government employee, I believe. I ordered dividers online from Wal-Mart that separated the room for privacy. Our showers and bathroom was a small walk from my hooch, maybe 50-100 meters or so away. The best thing about my hooch was its proximity to Route Irish, which was about a hundred meters or so away. At that time, Route Irish was a highway in the center of Baghdad, and considered the most dangerous highway in the world. So why would being in such close proximity to the most dangerous road in the world be considered a good thing? Well, I will explain, but you may still find my logic to be flawed at best. You see, when AQI and local insurgents would stop along the road just outside base and fire off mortar rounds, the mortars would go about a half mile or so, and had limited targeting capabilities. There primary targets were Aw-Faw Palace and the DFAC. What that meant was the mortars would fly right over me, so close in fact you could hear their very distinct whistle, like a big bottle rocket. This once considered prime location, became a not so prime location a few months after I got there due to the new CRAM, or Counter Rocket and Mortar defense system. A truly amazing weapon that was known on the Navy ships it originated from as the Phalanx. It was a massive machine gun which targeted incoming mortar rounds with very large explosive tipped bullets at about 3000 rounds per minute. They were very effective at stopping incoming mortars, but exactly how effective remains classified. But for me, the problem is that sometimes, they would not actually destroy the mortar in flight, but rather it would break it apart. When that started happening, the mortars would just drop, and my "apartment," was directly under its flight path. That sucked, at least from my perspective, and resulted in some pretty close calls. The large "T" walls were installed around each trailer, so unless it fell into your trailer, you would be stressed mentally, but physically you would be fine.

My hooch had a limited connection with the only internet option available call "Jackal." It was named after a type of wild dog you will find frequently roaming the camp. Oddly enough, on a slightly off topic post here, a Jackal actually ran off with the left boot of a new pair of boots I purchased the day earlier. My new boots had gotten wet and muddy, and I left them outside our office to dry. The only thing left was one of my boots, and a set of Jackal footprints as evidence of the crime. I saw a Jackal puppy playing with something in a nearby field a few days later, and I imagined it was likely my brand new left boot.

But anyway, moving on. The Jackal internet service provider was very expensive and provided only minimum bandwidth speeds. My internet access through Jackal was rarely enough for Skype calls home to your family, or streaming online videos. Having just been deployed to Afghanistan, and knowing there would likely be limited internet in Iraq, I purchased a SlingBox prior to leaving Florida, and with the low bandwidth settings I was able to watch my programs from back home on my off hours back in my hooch. That said, I could only view it in a very small window on my computer. Even better was my ability now to change the channel remotely on our cable TV back home. This provided me with great enjoyment when I would change the cartoons my kids were watching back home, to CNN or FOX news. It would almost certainly get an online response from whoever was watching the TV with something like, "come on dad, would you stop changing the channel." This seems like a silly thing, but it is that "touch of home" I referred to earlier that could take even your worst day, and make everything better.

The Awakening

Prior to deploying to Iraq, I reached out to my friend and former colleague, Aaron Baker. He was one of the most skilled coders and IT guys I have ever known. Computers were in Aaron's blood, as his dad had worked for years in the IT field, and as I understand, even somehow helped to pioneer one of the original audio chipsets. Unlike the tactical combat role I supported in Afghanistan, my job in Iraq was really something very new and exciting. We were pioneering a new field that the Army was just getting involved with on a tactical level. The Army calls it "Interactive Internet Activities", or IIA. What I did in Iraq was extremely classified and I will not acknowledge or discuss any procedures or processes involved with our mission.

Our IO mission was in support of the JPOTF, which stands for Joint Psychological Operations Task Force, and is pronounced "Japotif", in case you're wondering. PSYOP, or Psychological Operations, was previously known as Psychological Warfare until someone decided that warfare sounded to "warrish" for a military organization, and they renamed it to "Operations" to make it sound friendlier, I guess? Traditionally, you would associate this group of high speed soldiers with leaflet drops over enemy territory, but with the invention of the internet and social media, it was only a matter of time before the PSYOP community became more environmentally friendly and started shifting their focus from mass littering to spam. IIA, or Interactive Internet Activity, is about using the internet and social media to change hearts and minds, instead of bullets and bombs. It was a noble concept for an organization such as the U.S. Military. I liked the idea of using a tactical, targeted, social media approach much better than blowing people up. In fact, without implying how, I would argue that the efforts of the JPOTF, and our team, played a large part in reducing the bombings and violence in Iraq.

The Sunni and Shia have been fighting and killing each other for centuries, and if not for Saddam Hussain and his brutal control through the Baath Party (mostly Sunni), they would have continued. Sunni and Shia were kept at bay from each other and allowed to live together in "relative" peace. Although more Sunni than Shia, the bath party was meant as a cross-sectarian/religion organization, even allowing Christian and Catholic schools to teach in Iraq, which was unique to that entire, jacked up region. Once Saddam was removed from this equation, all bets were off, and the fighting between the Sunni and Shia began again, only this time with the U.S. military stuck in the middle of it. Shia, looking for payback, would kill Sunni, (and some Americans when they felt like it) and Sunni were killing Shia and Americans. A Sunni based faction formed called AQI, or Al-Qaida in Iraq, and was pretty much killing everyone. A handful of Sunni Clerics stepped up and formed an alliance with the

U.S., and the Sunni Awakening, or Al-Sahawa, was born. Basically, the U.S. was paying about 100,000 Sunni, many former Baathist, to work with us guarding checkpoints and collecting intelligence. And people say you can't buy love.

The new Shia led government didn't trust the Sunni, and felt that with the U.S. arming them, they would become a threat if legitimized. After the brutality of Saddam's regime against the Shia, you can't really blame them. But I personally knew several Shia that were just fine with the way things were under Saddam. Their kids went to Christian schools, and as long as you followed Saddam's rules, things were not that bad. FYI, Iran is mostly Shia. It's an alphabet soup of disorganized religion in that entire region over there, and if you can keep it all straight, well good on you. Heck, I likely screwed up in the description I just gave. Don't forget, I was and IT guy, not an analyst or historian. But I was there, so if you want to correct me and wasn't there, please feel free to do so, then kiss my ass ☺

As pissed as I was that McCain wanted to send in more troops, I thought it was a huge mistake for Obama to pull our troops out of there like he did. I cannot say how, but I knew our government leaders knew the Iraqi government would not accept the Sons of Iraq, and sure enough, they didn't. And that, my friends, is how ISIL was born. Just as fast as the U.S. stopped paying the members of the Sunni Awakening the monthly salary of just a few hundred dollars, ISIL enlistment skyrocketed. It was a good investment for the U.S., I mean think about it. You could pay 1,000 Sunni not to kill anyone and guard local neighborhoods for a month, for less than what my yearly salary alone was as a contractor. Just think of them as low-cost security guards and your hiring them as contractors. Perhaps Donald Trump's suggestion of taking their oil revenue and using it wasn't a bad idea after all. Use the oil money to pay the Sunni not to kill. Is it the most ideal solution? I doubt it. Would it have worked? I don't think most people are inclined to kill the person that signs their check each month.

The Sons of Iraq were mostly just good men that wanted to help, and didn't want to see their country torn apart by war. In October 2015, a Special Forces soldier with the 82nd airborne division was killed in a rescue mission in Iraq. The mission involved rescuing about 200 Iraqi that were about to be executed by

ISIL, and when the news reported that 20 of those rescued were Sons of Iraq members, my heart just dropped in my chest. I knew at that moment, this soldier died in the line of duty rescuing good people that are truly fighting for their country. Although the death of any U.S. soldier is tragic, to that soldier, he died with honor, far as I am concerned. I had heard the Sons of Iraq had all but disappeared, and it made me feel good to hear that at least small groups of them are still fighting for their country back in Iraq.

Interactive Internet Activities (IIA)

Information Operations (IO) Joint Publication 3-13.2, Psychological Operations, dated 07 January, 2010, defines Interactive Internet Activities (IIA) as follows: (a) Psychological Operations and Computer Network Operations. CNO support PSYOP with dissemination assets to include interactive Internet activities. CNO activities can deny or degrade an adversary's ability to access, report, and process information. This capability supports PSYOP by providing access to digital media within the information environment to reach intended targets.
[http://fas.org/irp/doddir/dod/jp3-13-2.pdf]

So how did the JPOTF and our team fit in all of this? Even with an infrastructure that was pretty well banged up, most of the Iraqi people still had internet. They would chat, blog, and share their thoughts on social media sites. It is public knowledge that the U.S. military had setup Iraqi news websites, blogs and other social media sites. Before you think that I am spilling some sort of classified information, on every site, usually hidden and in small fonts, these sites would state somewhere that it was owned by the U.S. Department of Defense. These sites are designed to look normal, just like any other site. The use of such sites is well documented and has been reported on in numerous occasions and publicly available on DoD Public Affairs websites.

My job was really very simple for the JPOTF, and involved maintaining a database, SharePoint collaboration site, 7 laptops, and an un-attributable "dirty" network. Seriously, it was a huge waste of taxpayer dollars, and I was never shy about telling them so on my contract. That is all that I can say about what my responsibilities were for the military while in Iraq. I took an oath when I was granted my clearance, and breaking that oath will never be up for consideration.

What I would like to discuss is the potential use of IIA on social media by both corporations and foreign governments. It is a field for which I am considered by many as a subject matter expert in. IIA, and its potential tactical use in social media and socially engineered warfare, should be considered a true threat to national security. It is one of my greatest hopes in this book that people understand the potential threat an application like this can have.

You will remember when I ran for Pasco county Election Supervisor and tried to warn the residents of Pasco, and of all Florida, to the stupidity of going with touch screen voting machines so early in their development. Nobody listened to me, even after $10's of millions in taxpayer dollars was literally thrown into a recycling shredder. This doesn't leave me with much hope that anyone will listen to me when I warn them about the threat of IIA and socially engineer warfare affecting the outcome of a presidential election. Let's see what will happen this time.

During my time in Iraq, I helped pioneer the development of new IIA applications, though I will neither confirm nor deny anything I was potentially involved in as it relates to our mission in

Iraq. I am using the IIA skills I learned during my time with Dynology, to teach people on how to protect themselves while using social media. I believe foreign nations are developing similar applications, even those with defensive capabilities, at a very rapid pace as well. This is likely due to the inexpensive price tag for such a powerful weapon. What do I mean about defensive IIA capabilities? Imagine if 100,000 fake personas of terrorists appeared on social media making false claims, all to distract emergency services from their real target; a large, coordinated attack. Defensive IIA would potentially employ analysts with algorithms which could help weed out such an IIA operation.

If I were to build the perfect IIA social media application, I would want to give it the ability for teams of analysts to collaborate internally, while they participate in chat rooms and other online discussions in real-time. Using commercially available proxy services such as TOR, along with VM's (virtual machines), I would setup workstation to make it look like we were chatting with them from anywhere in the world I wanted them to think I was. I could also reach out to private companies that specialized in anonymizing a person's online presence, which could literally provide me with a physical, IP presence almost anywhere in the world - for the right price. And before you ask, yes, such companies do exist, and the cost of these services could run from the hundreds of thousands of dollars, into the millions. I would argue the COTS version, which was free, provides the same if not better anonymizing capabilities.

But again, when you're the U.S. government, why do something logical for free, when you can do the same thing spending millions of tax-payer appropriate dollars? This is the mentality of our government, or haven't you been paying attention. Anonymity is essential because if a moderator, for example, on an extremist site with known ties to terrorist organizations, tried to look at IP's of the "personas" the analysts were using in the chat rooms, they would not be able to tell where we truly were. Using a commercial internet service provider, or what is called in the industry a "Dirty ISP" network, at any given time you could have one person (analysts) having a discussion as ten, twenty, thirty or more different "personas," or fake identities. This further supports my position that sending me to Iraq, when I specialize in un-attributable "dirty" networks capable of making me appear as being anywhere in the world, was a huge waste of taxpayers' money in a very ironic way.

Back to the subject of the covert, tactical use of IIA, you could have arguments taking place to represent both sides of a discussion, and have the same person appearing to be two, three, twenty or however many different people you wanted. All of these personas could be arguing dozens of different points, which would bring our targets (the general public) into the discussion. Once others were involved in the discussions, you could inject fake news media reports which you created, which would help to influence others in these radical chat rooms that were thinking about strapping on suicide vests, not to do it. A bonus to this is that by linking these discussions, and all of the people exchanging links, you would increase what is known as "search engine optimization," or SEO's. What that did was made it so your "product" or discussion would show up at the top of most major search engines such as Google and others. Think about the value in having your product show up in the top three choices when people are searching for a product like a new appliance or satellite provider. (Shout-out to my man, Cordes Owen :-) Imagine the impact an IIA program could have had on Omar Mateen, the Orlando shooter. A properly ran program could have spotted Omar online, and either de-radicalized him, or monitored his behavior more closely. Radical Islamic terrorists cannot as easily reach the U.S. border without using social media as effectively as they have. Which do you think is more likely to be successful, an IIA program as described above, or taking away the 2nd Amendment and the 300 million plus guns in the U.S? Even if the U.S. government made people think they were doing it, when they really wouldn't, would it have a deterring effect? Sort of like when Regan made the Russians think we were building a Star Wars project in space. This eventually contributed to the fall of the Soviet Union financially, or so I was told in the history books.

There is nothing new about the techniques used in IIA which I described earlier, it is nothing different than two cops playing good cop, bad cop in an undercover sting operation. Except in my system, you only needed one cop to play all parts, good cop, bad cop and even a few bad guys if the situation warranted to gain peoples trust. Now, a staff of 1000 people would have the power and influence of 50,000. At the end of each shift, when analyst would log out of their computers, the virtual image would be restored to its factory default settings, removing any conversations, notes, possible key logging software or other malware that could have been picked up on a terrorist affiliated site. While, everything that took place, like the conversations, multi-media uploads, analyst interpretations and assessments could be documented in a secure database and easily queried for tactical dissemination, lawyers and peer review later. You could filter your results in the database by religion, race, income bracket, location and politics (based on IP's). Really just about anything.

The analysts could make comments, and conversations can be flagged for review by larger teams and lawyers. What IIA could potentially be used for in commercial applications, and for this discussion, bears listening very closely too. What's equally important to everything already discussed, is that people understand that the tactical use of IIA on social media and network news, can be done. Not only can it be done, I am exceptionally confident is has been used, and is still being used by countries hostile to U.S. interests. And I am not just referring to the Russians, Hillary! They all use it. Major corporations and even U.S. political campaigns have likely used similar, if not even more advanced operational applications of IIA as I previously described. Are you starting to become just a little concerned about now?

I believe because I helped to design and build this stuff, I can spot it more easily. That said, by its very nature, the tactical use of IIA is almost impossible to prove unless you catch someone directly in the act, or possibly a financial trail. I personally believe, with a very high degree of confidence, that on 11/14/2015, during the democratic debate in Iowa, a tactical IIA operation was being used to target specific candidates through Twitter feeds. Some was likely picked up and used by major media news outlets as real. I will not say who I think was doing it, because I cannot prove it. I will say that the candidate(s) which are most unlikely to be doing well, yet are on top in polling and have a very strong and well organized social media campaign - in both parties - would be a good place to start looking. And yes, I intentionally described more than one candidate.

I sometimes wonder how many U.S. soldiers or Iraqi citizens are alive today because of the use of different forms of IIA. How many people were ready to strap on a suicide vest, or setup a roadside bomb didn't because of IIA? How many Sunni men joined the Sons of Iraq and fought with the U.S., rather than taking up arms against us with AIQ because of IIA? These numbers are impossible to calculate, but in a recent social media test performed by Facebook, they stated that through manipulation of postings strategically placed on their member's profiles based on their identifiable political leanings, Facebook influenced the outcome of an election in 2012 through increased voter turnout in targeted voting precincts.

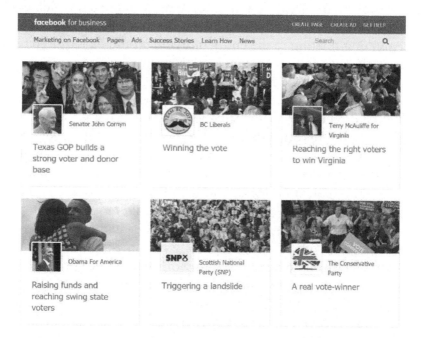

[http://www.wsj.com/articles/furor-erupts-over-facebook-experiment-on-users-1404085840] Obviously, if you increase voter turnout in a democratic precinct, and keep voters home in a republican precinct, you are going to affect the outcome of that election. Facebook actually publicly announced that they had successfully affected the voter turnout in a specific race. To me, that is a very scary thought. It literally threatens the very core of our democracy, which is voting. Even Vladimir Putin has commented on how corporations, money and political influence has controlled our election process. How long will it be until corporations find it is easier to pay a social media network like Facebook to influence an election, than it is to lobby congress to get a law passed? Or has it already begun...?

It's The Corporations, Stupid!

As I have said several times before, I cannot discuss what we were doing in Iraq, but I will say everything I was involved with was exceptionally monitored and controlled by teams of lawyers and officers. It is the stated policy of the Department of Defense that, if there was even the slightest hint of an American citizen which could be influenced by the DoA's socially engineered IIA, all bets were off. Anything relating to the entity or event would be required to immediately end, and all documentation destroyed.

Nothing we could do could have ANY possible effect in influencing a U.S. citizen in ANY way. It was one of the highest operational directives I would say the JPOTF had. It is also a bit complicated, but If you understand servers, then you understand an Iraqi website spewing terrorist propaganda could easily be legally hosted on a server farm in Tampa, and not technically be violating any laws. Any potential interaction with Iraqi's on a website that is merely hosted on a server within the U.S., could require hours, potentially days of discussions and legal battles within the government. Now there are other U.S. government organizations that theoretically could be allowed to work within the confines I describe here that might involve U.S. citizens, but the U.S. military is STRICTLY prohibited from doing so.

I was always very impressed with such checks and balances within the DoD policy. Even those people whom were prone to ignoring policy, gave going around this one a wide berth. It is for this reason that unlike Edward Snowden, I have trust in our government as a whole. Snowden would like you to believe that some GS 9 sitting at his desk somewhere in South Dakota is drinking coffee and randomly listening in on your conversation with your old high school friend about that fine Bubba Kush you just smoked, and that is simply not the case. To make my point, when is the last time you ever saw any government agency do anything without a ridiculous amount of bureaucratic bullshit? I apologize for the use of a bad word here, as my kids are likely to read this book someday. That said, sometimes politically correct wording doesn't give what you are describing the appropriate level of attention. Your local government can't order toilet paper for their office without doing an environmental study on the impact different brands may have on some of the local critters. Seriously, our government has struggled to get ahead of the information Snowden released. All they ever needed to do was create an environment that showed support from our leadership, and too be better examples in their compliance to existing policy.

To me, the other true threat to our nation's security comes from the Military Industrial Complex, which doesn't have to play by these rules. There are few laws to stop them, or even punish them if they were caught in the act. This is something the Clinton's have never seem to understand, because they never had to pay for it, the taxpayers did. It is the "rule" in our government and MIC, and as you will read later with my time in South Korea, not the "exception."

The use of IIA is likely the only truly effective weapon we have in the war on terror from within our U.S. borders. How can we ever expect to be able to win this war if we cannot control the fraud, waste, and abuse between the MIC's and our government – especially our leadership? If not intentional, it works well for our government leadership and the MIC community to distract people.

What American's need to be afraid of is not what our government is doing with the collection of data, because everything I saw was a very detailed and thorough series of checks and balances to ensure constitutional compliance. What American's need to think about is what private companies like Leoni, MPRI, Dynology, G4S, Facebook, Twitter and others are doing. Some, like I mentioned earlier with Facebook, are openly and admittedly experimenting with different forms of IIA right now! All it would take is for China, Russia, Iran, or North Korea getting dirt on some high-level executive with administrative access to Facebook's user's data, and being blackmailed into influencing the outcome of a presidential election. Better yet, instigate riots and uprisings like we saw with Michael Brown, which has turned into the Black Lives Matters movement.

I would almost guarantee that one or more countries with hostile intentions towards western culture, were using IIA to influence social media in the riots we saw surrounding Michael Brown. And I would bet my bottom dollar that political campaigns, beverage companies and lobbyists are also employing similar techniques I helped to pioneer in Iraq, only by now far more advanced and automated. In fact, I have seen several instances where I recognized it, like I mentioned earlier with the democratic debates. How in the world American's have such distrust in their government, but have seemingly complete faith in private companies and political campaigns is simply beyond me? Actually, I do know how and it likely involves the very same tactical use of IIA I have been talking about. To make matters worse, our election process is totally integrating itself in social media like never before. This holistic, nearly symbiotic relationship between broadcast media and social media is frightening to me. Again, not by our government, but by our adversaries. Is there proof that other countries are doing this? Just yesterday the FCC announced they are investigating a Baltimore radio station spewing pro-China propaganda that apparently has a 60% ownership by the Chinese government. This is just your standard, old school PSYOP, not IIA. But if they aren't doing it, then they are complete idiots because they should be. You cannot fault your enemy from exploiting such an obvious weakness. We can only fault ourselves for not being prepared. I would do it if I were them. It's cheap, easy, and people are basically very easily manipulated. If you blindly trust anything you see or hear on the internet, you are an idiot! Brave men and women have given blood and tremendous sacrifice for the freedom and democracy we enjoy in this country, and if you don't respect it and protect it, you don't deserve it, and you will most likely lose it. The only way I see of preventing it, is by broadcast media and the larger social media companies requiring people to authenticate their identities. I just don't see that happening, even if it means the end of our democracy as we know it. This authentication and verification is something you will read about later in my book where I startup a veteran based non-profit.

If used correctly and for its intended purpose, IIA could actually be used to prevent wars, fight terrorism and protect those that cannot protect themselves - without ever firing a single shot.

The ISIL inspired attack in Orlando by Omar Mateen is a prime example of terrorism that IIA could have likely prevented. I personally offer what I call "Ethical IIA" services today, strictly to non-governmental organizations that help people that are otherwise oppressed, or targeted by groups that seek to harm women and children through human trafficking in impoverished nations. The internet can be used for good, or as a weapon capable of mass destruction the likes of which even Oppenheim couldn't have imagined. And the worst thing of all is that nobody would know what happened until it was too late, if they ever knew it happened at all.

In the category of a bad idea gone wrong, someone thought it was a great idea to engineer a virus that would specifically target Iran's nuclear power plant which was being used for uranium production, and then again to target their oil ministry. Yet in just a few months' time, it was reverse engineered by Iran, and a virus with similar characteristics was used against Saudi Arabia's Aramco Oil Company, destroying a reported 50,000 computer hard drives, and leaving an image of a burning American flag as a screensaver.

Having the ability to do something doesn't always mean it is a good idea to do it. Such an attack is obvious, and almost assures retaliation. I would argue that using IIA to alter the outcome of the next Iranian election through anonymized proxy servers, IIA and socially engineer warfare, would be a far more powerful tool in our toolbox. Nobody would ever retaliate, because nobody would ever know or could prove it even happened. It's like a virus that kills its host, then destroys itself and all possible evidence that could lead back to it. Like I said before, I am certain other countries are already doing this, and it is very likely that the 2016 presidential election in the U.S. has already been targeted by one or more countries hostile to U.S. interests, and even by political operatives within our country seeking political gain. Right now, I believe there are huge, well-funded government offices in China, North Korea, Iran, Russia and other countries with rooms filled with hundreds, possibly thousands of English speaking foreign nationals that are monitoring literally everything on the most popular U.S. social media sites. These intelligence analysts are using multiple personas that are designed to engage American citizens in chat rooms, blogs, and through multi-media "memes" in a tactical and coordinated effort to destabilize the

U.S. and our allies. They will be using tactical IIA through anonymizing proxy servers and other tools that allow them to appear as though they are right across the street from you, if they so desire. Making matters worse, U.S. news agencies have now incorporated social media into their broadcasts, making internet chatter and actual reporting of news virtually indistinguishable from each other. I was watching social media during the Michael Brown incident and could see very subtle signs of such foreign influence in the very chat rooms and blogs that were fueling the flames. Errors in grammar you would find in Russian or Ukrainian culture, (I was briefly married to a Russian women) and the re-use or copy and pasting of the same or similar questions and comments across multiple blog sites by the same people, using different personas, was evident to me. The naming conventions used in their personas are also sometimes clues. These are hard to spot by their very design, but I could detect the telltale signs of an organized and coordinated, tactical IIA operation. Even if I had access to the hosting servers, I would not be able to confidently trace back the origin of the user making the posts, because they would have in place simple proxy services that would make it look like they were coming from right where they say they were from. Organizations have, and will continue going to great lengths to do this, sometimes purchasing apartments and setting up a small server with just enough data capabilities to host a proxy service and route traffic when needed, just to mask the geo-locations of their analysts. The cost of this is minimal for most countries I listed. How hard do you think this would be financially for Russia or China to setup in the U.S.? Russia maintains one of the largest criminal cyber networks in the world, called the RBN, or Russian Business Network. Through this network, millions of unprotected computers in the U.S. are infected and controlled by malware. How hard would it be for any size country or organization to purchase proxy services through organizations affiliated with the RBN? If you were a terrorist, what would you rather have? 1 thermonuclear warhead that would make one big boom, or an IIA program that would allow you to alter a U.S. presidential election, and nobody would ever know it happened? For one, I am nearly certain the cost of a thermonuclear warhead would be far greater than the $33 million I project it would cost to run a successful IIA program sufficient to alter a U.S. presidential election. I also believe IIA could do more damage to our nation, as a whole, than a nuclear weapon. Using IIA to start riots in cities across the U.S., destabilize the U.S. economy, and turn our allies into enemies, would cause more damage. I wonder if anyone is listening to me now? Probably not.

If my run for Elections Supervisor is any indication, people just don't pay attention. I wish I was wrong, but I am not. My brain seems to naturally work in such a way that I see these things when others cannot. The only way to stop this from happening is to either A: stop using social media, or switch to a secure, user verified service like what I have built for veterans with my non-profit organization, which is not going to happen, or B: stop blindly trusting what you read online and do some research yourself. Don't respond emotionally to what you see before you understand the situation better. That "count to ten" thing you would told when you got angry as a child, would go a long way towards making IIA far less effective to foreign interests that seek to harm our country. Oh, and how about trusting your government a little more, and private companies a lot less. I make that last comment with some reservation, as our government has simply become far to close and dependent on the military industrial complex. Take a look at Craigslist or most any job marketplace out there and all you see are corporations within the military industrial complex hiring our best and brightest military for their training and clearances, just to sell their services back to our government at triple or quadruple the price. It's insane really.

Even with all the internal stupidity, fraud, waste and abuse within our government, the oversight and regulatory restrictions our government agencies have makes using IIA against our own people virtually useless. Russia, China, Iran and private corporations don't have these same restrictions, and can initiate an IIA operation with ease and great efficiency. If the U.S. government ever tried to use IIA to affect an operation in real time like the Michael Brown issue, by the time the lawyers and the half dozen other bureaucrats finally came to some agreement, the event would already be over. People, you know this is true. You know how the U.S. government works. The intellectual standards of the people running your local driver's license office, are the same people working as GS employees for the Federal Government, and running these agencies.

When I detail my time in Korea working with GS employees at the directorate, general officers, and staff level, you will understand how I come to this conclusion even better. IIA operations outside the U.S. could be very simple for our government and military, because there are little or no constitutional constraints we need to be worried about. Even then, our military still operates with all the bureaucracy you would expect from our government. I like to say our military is "efficiently inefficient." We need to take the military industrial complex out of combat zones completely. They have their role back in the states, developing new technologies, training our troops and some logistical roles. But in combat zones, we need to have military only. For those in the military thinking about a career in contracting, we need to have at least a two to five-year moratorium before you can go to work for the military industrial complex, and draw these well-trained military personnel into government jobs, while eliminating those whom have never served in the military from GS positions. Most government contracting companies prohibit employees from leaving to work for competing companies. My company, Dynology, required me to sign a non-compete agreement, which I initially refused until language was included that allowed me to work for the veteran's non-profit I founded.

Dynology has branched off into another company named, ClearForce, and in my opinion, poses a direct threat to our country at the highest levels.

Deep State "Predictive" Social Media Behavioral Threat Software

ClearForce is a family owned business, founded by Ret. 4-Star Marine Corp General James Jones. A lifelong friend of John McCain and a Republican, Jones also served as President Obama's National Security Advisor. Ret. General Michael Hayden, former director of the CIA, recently joined the board. The Deep State can operate outside the government as part of the Military Industrial Complex, without all the rules of a government agency.

CLEARFORCE

Insider Risk | Industry Solutions | Benefits | News & Information | About Us | Contact

General James L. Jones, USMC, Ret.

General James Logan Jones, Jr. is a former United States National Security Advisor to President Obama and a retired United States Marine Corps General. During his military career, he served as Commander, United States European Command and Supreme Allied Commander Europe from 2003 to 2006 and as the 32nd Commandant of the Marine Corps from July 1999 to January 2003. Jones retired from the Marine Corps in February of 2007 after 40 years of service. In November 2007, he was appointed by the U.S. Secretary of State as special envoy for Middle East security. General Jones served as chairman of the Atlantic Council from June 2007 to January 2009, when he assumed the post of National Security Advisor that he held until November 2010. General Jones has also served on the Boards of Invacare Corporation, Boeing Company, Chevron Corporation and General Dynamics.

James L. Jones, III, Founder & Executive Chairman

James L. Jones III (Jim) is the Executive Chairman and former Chief Executive Officer of Dynology Corporation, a prominent IT firm headquartered in Tyson's Corner, VA. Serving as Dynology's Chief Executive, Jim has 20+ years of experience in strategic communications, security, cyber and virtualization technologies, driving more than $50M of highly successful IT initiatives to organizations within the commercial sector, DoD and other Federal Agencies. Mr. Jones served as Chairman of the 2011 Fight Night on behalf of Fight for Children, is a long-time member of the Marine Corps Law Enforcement Foundation (MCLEF), has worked with the Armed Services YMCA (ASYMCA) eventually working for the organization to enhance their web presence, and the Tragedy Assistance Program for Survivors (TAPS) organization in helping to raise awareness and funds for the survivor families that carry on the legacies of those who made the ultimate sacrifice.

General Michael Hayden

General Michael Hayden former Director of the Central Intelligence Agency. Before becoming Director of CIA, General Hayden served as the country's first Principal Deputy Director of National Intelligence and was the highest-ranking intelligence officer in the armed forces. Earlier, he served as Director of the National Security Agency. Currently, he serves as a principal at The Chertoff Group, a security and risk management advisory firm, and as a Distinguished Visiting Professor at George Mason University. In 2014, he was the inaugural Humanitas Visiting Professor in Intelligence Studies at Oxford University in the United Kingdom. His recent book, playing to the Edge: American Intelligence in the Age of Terror, was a New York Times best seller and was recently selected as one of the 100 most notable books of 2016.

"ClearForce delivers a complete integrated solution that protects organizations and employees from insider threat by *continually evaluating leading indicators of high risk behavior, emotional and financial stress in and outside the workplace…* our solution is fully integrated and automated."

"DoD – NISPOM Change 2 - The Defense Security Service's Conforming Change 2 to DoD 5220.22-M, National Industrial Security Program Operating Manual (NISPOM) and an accompanying Industrial Security Letter were released on 18 May 2016."

CLEARFORCE

Insider Risk | Industry Solutions | Benefits | News & Information | About Us | Contact

DoD – NISPOM Change 2

The Defense Security Service's Conforming Change 2 to DoD 5220.22-M, National Industrial Security Program Operating Manual (NISPOM) and an accompanying Industrial Security Letter were released on 18 May 2016.

Among other changes, the updates require that DoD-cleared contractors implement an insider threat program. Contractors had until 30 November 2016 to self-certify compliance with new guidelines. DSS is currently employing anew 21 question checklist to ensure compliance with this requirement.

Specifically, the NISPOM states: "Defense Security Service (DSS) to require that all entities possessing a facility clearance/cleared personnel shall incorporate insider threat based technologies and processes to maintain their current ability to hold clearances." The four referenced processes are:

* Designate Insider Threat Program Manager

* Provide Employee Insider Threat Training Within First 30 Days

Recent changes to NISPOM are timed perfectly with this unprecedented level of classified information being leaked, and the grand opening of ClearForce. Coincidence? Many of the changes in NISPOM were influenced by policies of both General Jones and John McCain. Gen. Jones, stands to profit heavily in providing compliance solutions through ClearForce. John McCain?

What should concern everyone is the potential of a company to reshape the structure of our government, intelligence and defense agencies, to fit the psychological requirements of John McCain or General Jones. These are two of the most powerful people in the highest levels of our government and intelligence communities!

To me, based on motive, means and access, they should be two of the highest suspects on the list of possible leakers. Imagine if that were the case, and they used the leaks they blame on liberals, as justification to begin a purge of those that fit the ClearForce psychological and behavioral threat profiles (see below.)

⬙ CLEARFORCE

Insider Risk | Industry Solutions | Benefits | News & Information | About Us | Contact

The Problem

Insider threats are a major component of cyber risk and workplace crime. Research indicates that more than half of corporate losses from cyber threats involve insiders who initiate or participate in these crimes. Insider crime can also include fraud, theft of real or intellectual property, as well as workplace violence.

Simply consider the challenges that make a trusted employee vulnerable to blackmail or coercion; a need for money for a family crisis, spiraling debt resulting from an unknown gambling addiction or perhaps a sudden medical emergency or recent divorce, college tuition, elderly care. Or the employee who was arrested for felony or a pattern of misdemeanor crime that has gone unreported.

Now consider the amount of personal information that is swirling around in public databases or on the Dark Web. At first glance it might seem harmless and scattered, but in the hands of bad actors they profile and discover who they need to coerce to carry them past your cyber perimeter.

Most of this unseen behavior takes place away from work, which accounts for about 60% of your employee's activity. These high-risk behaviors have been proven to drive good employees to take advantage of their inside access for personal gain or to fix a stressful situation through workplace misconduct or crime.

"The Problem," as seen by ClearForce, can be fixed through highly invasive, real-time monitoring of employees, both at work, and at home. With real-time monitoring of a security cleared government employee or contractor's social media, banking, driving, dating, dark web, sickness in family, the potential for abuse is astronomical. This is just some of the personal information that could be used to assess potential threats for leaks which could jeopardize national security based on pre-defined values. If you think this is a good idea, you better hope the guy you voted for is the one responsible for establishing a baseline for those values. As it stands, John McCain and Obama's former National Security Advisor will be setting the parameters for any potential liberal "culling."

"Simply consider the challenges that make a trusted employee vulnerable to blackmail or coercion; a need for money for a family crisis, spiraling debt resulting from an unknown gambling addiction or perhaps a sudden medical emergency or recent divorce, college tuition, elderly care. Or the employee who was arrested for felony or a pattern of misdemeanor crime that has gone unreported."

*"ClearForce delivers a complete integrated solution that protects organizations and employees from insider threat by continually evaluating leading indicators of high risk behavior, **emotional and financial stress in and outside the workplace**. Because our solution is fully integrated and automated."*

Per NISPOM guidelines, compliance requirements began in late 2016. It was largely portrayed as an attempt to reduce future "Edward Snowden" type leaks. Changes were also made to whistleblower laws that same year in 2013, which would likely have a far greater impact in reducing the threat of leaking, but the changes were all just window dressing. The DC swamp won that round.

Not only has ClearForce uniquely positioned themselves to meet the requirements for contractors and government with their new, predictive analytics, there is nothing to stop them from classifying liberal leaning political views as a potential threat, and filter them out, much like the IRS did with patriots. The key difference is that the IRS has oversight, and a private company does not. Such preemptive threat measures are already mandated by NISPOM, but consider the scenario where an employer wants to know which employees have liberal political views, then proceeds to selectively terminate for pretty much any reason they want. They could easily point to the ClearForce emotional and behavioral threat assessment as their justification for termination. Feel free to keep talking about the Trump/Russia narrative, while these folks can operate with virtual impunity.

The Keys to the Kingdom

When I first arrived in Iraq, the program was being run by LTC Whatley, one of the finest officers I ever had the privilege to work for. He was very good at his job, and also had a fun sense of humor. His leadership was something you just don't find very often in the military, and makes for a great working environment. Do your job right, and LTC Whatley didn't hassle you. Screw up, and he would let you know.

It was right around Christmas time and LTC Whatley was being transferred back to the states. By now I was watching my SlingBox in full screen mode, which is a story you will read about in a few minutes, but other than that, I can't really say anything had changed, and there was little if anything for me to do. I won't say who was responsible because it was a direct violation of General Order number one, but we were treated to the most wonderful bottle of scotch on Christmas Eve, and put up the movie "Team America" on the big screen TV in our office as our holiday movie. It is a big deal if you got busted with liquor of any kind while deployed, which made it taste even better. I was told the liquor was procured at the Embassy in the Green Zone. I was also told the State Department folks at the Embassy in the Green Zone could drink, which seemed just more than a bit hypocritical to me. I don't know the accuracy to my last statement that State Department folks were authorized to drink, I just know that this was something I was told. Service members were strictly prohibited under General Order #1.

Now, getting back on track.

The "Keys to the Kingdom," was what LTC Whatley referred to as our ability to do our job, without the bureaucracy that continually tied our hands. It was something LTC Whatley aspired for, but never actually got. I made this mock photo for LTC Whatley when he was preparing to PCS back to the states as a going away gift.

My contract in Iraq was for 1 year with a salary, including bonuses, of nearly $240,000. There was a reason that subject matter experts were paid such a healthy amount of money, and that was because it was a really, really, dangerous place to be. But the sad thing was that I never needed to really be there other than for a few days to initially set things up. If indeed I ever needed any physical presence to have performed my required deliverables, everything could have easily been remotely administered from pretty much anywhere in the world. Once I had setup the server and roughly 10 brand new laptops, there was really nothing for me to do. I just sat around watching TV, while automated programs monitored and protected our services. Physically installing the 10 laptops could easily have been performed by an enlisted soldier certified as an IMO (Information Management Officer.) Servers can now be securely operated in the "cloud" environment, or controlled remotely through a secure connection from my bedroom back in the states. To make this story of fraud, waste, and abuse even worse, my friend Aaron Baker was hired on, granted an interim Top-Secret clearance, and brought to Iraq so we could now have a 24 hour / 2 man physical presence. Again, no physical presence was ever necessary. I am reminded of that movie, Contact, with Jodie Foster, when she was

 talking with the guy that was contracted by the government to build the first portal machine. After the first machine was destroyed by the religious terrorist, and Foster thought all was lost, he reminded her of the government's philosophy that went something like "why build just one when you can have two for twice the cost." Aaron had come on board about 5 months into the contract, if memory serves me correct. Although he was an absolute computer genius, his physical presence was even less necessary than mine was.

Our building was called the "Sea huts", which was yet another project that had been hired out for local contractors to build, and they ran off with the money without completing it. The Seabees came in after and built us this fine establishment out of particle board. The Seabees really are an amazing and talented group of people. I still wonder if there was actually any job that the U.S. government hired local companies in either Iraq or Afghanistan to build, that was ever built as designed and contracted? In my personal experience, not one of the places I had worked in Iraq or Afghanistan was completed as per the requirements agreed upon in the contract deliverables by the local businesses we contracted to build.

As I am writing this book, I watched a few days ago a news report that was chastising Donald Trump for making a comment about how the military and contractors were stealing while in Iraq.

Trump: U.S. troops stole money in Iraq
By [Ben Schreckinger](#)
06/14/16 10:07 PM EDT
Updated 06/14/16 11:33 PM EDT
Donald Trump rang in the Army's 241st birthday in unusual fashion on Tuesday — by calling attention to theft of government funds by American soldiers in Iraq.
"Iraq, crooked as hell. How about bringing baskets of money — millions and millions of dollars — and handing it out?," Trump said at an evening rally. "I want to know who were the soldiers that had that job, because I think they're living very well right now, whoever they may be."
Read more: http://www.politico.com/story/2016/06/trump-us-troop-stole-millions-and-millions-in-iraq-224352#ixzz4BqQVX73n

To answer his question, I personally think many, if not most of these soldiers you were referring to are now working for the military industrial complex. As you will read below, I fully confess to my part in this sort of fraud, waste, and abuse. Eventually, I could not continue to be a part of it, and I believe it eventually resulted in the loss of my career. You can judge for yourself when you finish my book. This next story will support at least one example of the fraud, waste, and abuse Mr. Trump so un-artfully described.

I was provided a nice, private office where I would sit all day streaming my SlingBox that I had setup back home in the states before I left. Friday's were the best, when I could do this while enjoying all you can eat steak and lobster. I had a much better internet connection at the office than I had in my hooch, so I spent most of my time at the office. I had touched on that in the beginning of the book, and how I was approached when our annual funding requests came in for anything I needed to make the mission better. After repeatedly saying "no sir, everything is good on this end, sir. Don't need a thing," I was told directly to find something we could use, or we would lose this money in our next budget, and I would likely lose my job. You will quickly find in this business that if you are asked something twice by the government, or your company, you never give the same answer if you wanted to keep your job. So, I told them we could maybe use some more bandwidth on our dirty network. We didn't need it, and they all knew it, but it was the only thing I could think of, and a little more bandwidth would allow me to stream my SlingBox in full screen mode. A few days later they come back and tell me they ordered another couple of megabytes of dedicated satellite bandwidth, and that a local satellite ISP would be coming out to install our new satellite shortly. I had no idea how much a few megabytes of dedicated satellite bandwidth would cost in Iraq, but it came to something like over $350,000 for the year. They brought out and installed a huge, 3-meter disc on top of our bomb shelter. A small price to pay for being able to stream my TV shows from back home in full screen, don't you think?

Morale, Welfare, and Recreation

The food we were provided by KBR was fantastic. It was all you can eat and hosted an ice cream bar, breakfast bar and on Fridays, they served all you can eat steak and lobster - I kid you not! I would go in at get about six lobster tails, a bowl of butter and a nice fat steak to go and head back to my office. It was awesome! You could purchase illegal copies of DVD's with the newest movies for around six discs for $10 (or was it 10 discs for $6?) over at Camp Liberty right in front of the PX. I found this strange because they were competing with legal copies sold inside the base PX at full price for around $20.00 each. For the life of me I cannot understand how the commanding generals would walk right past this every day when they would go to the DFAC for chow, and not put a stop to it? Just goes to show the hypocrisy within our military leadership, and I think hurts their command ability because of it. Remember how they took away our TGI Friday's in Afghanistan, but not the illegal DVD's - which I reported as a direct threat to our national security. So, I eventually concluded that if you can't beat them, join them. That said, I would never put these DVD's in anything but my personal laptop, which I dedicated to watching these. I have never and would never put them in a government laptop or on a government network after what I saw in Afghanistan, which I discussed earlier. I knew better because of my IT background, but most everyone else did not. I would regularly find people watching illegal DVD's on government systems - connected to classified government networks. I got burned for speaking up about this in Afghanistan, and wasn't going to get burned again.

The USO provided a few events for us such as some golf pro's that came out to visit us at the grand opening of the new driving range they built behind the JPOTF. That was a pretty cool

day for sure. The Corps of Engineers built an amazing racetrack for remote controlled cars as well. I bought an RC car when I returned home on leave, and would frequently take my RC Desert Truck out to the track to kill time. You can go a little stir crazy after a year of being confined in a secure facility a few miles wide in the center of Baghdad, and these things made it a lot easier to cope with. You had to be careful though, because it was easy sometimes to forget where you were at. One moment your having fun at the RC track, and the next thing you know a large mortar round is landing a few hundred meters from your position, and the reality of living in war zone takes hold.

Living in a war zone was starting to take a toll on me emotionally, and I was really struggling mentally with an incident that happened in Afghanistan. I wasn't sleeping well at all, which was not helped by the stress of the mortars

and the constant sounds of combat helicopters and aircraft taking off and landing. I think it was about this time that my personal issues, which now I understand as likely being post-traumatic stress disorder, or PTSD, was starting to affect my marriage. I began waking up many nights with images in my head from dreams of what look like manikins scattered around a field with their arms, legs and other plastic manikin parts separated from their actual bodies by a few meters. They were all melting and on fire. I would awake from this dream every time after I would approach what I was sure were these plastic figures on the ground burning. People don't fall apart and burn like that, right? As I would approach the small objects on the ground, much like you would view something from those new augmented reality googles, I realized they were children, their arms and legs separated from their torso from the force of the blast, and burning from the heat of the explosions. In my nightmares, I see their faces, numbering over a hundred, then wake up and cannot fall back to sleep. Fortunately, that was just a dream, right... Everyone knows something like that could never happen without worldwide condemnation of such a mistake. I started to become indifferent to my life, at times not caring if I lived or died from one day to another. I remember one day at the office when the incoming alarm was sounding and everyone either ran to the bomb shelter, or took cover under a desk, while I just walked to the door to go outside and watch it. LTC Whatley screamed at me something to the effect "Bergy, have you lost your f*ing mind?" He may have been closer to the truth than he understood or meant. I didn't talk about this to anyone other than my doctor when I went home on leave, and he prescribed me valium to help me sleep.

Much of the work we were doing in Iraq, I was told, had never been done before by the Army, and that meant a lot of extra scrutiny was put on all of us.

I have four kids and I love them very much. Sometimes there are things you just need to overlook when you're in uniform, or as a contractor. I learned this lesson in the very beginning when I first deployed to Afghanistan, and brought to the attention of my command the issue with people watching illegal Chinese bootlegs of U.S. TV shows. But there are things that as a father, you just cannot overlook and need to report. This is one of those examples where I did my job, but leadership failed, and if I pushed it, would have been fired.

So, now that I am writing a book, I thought it would be a great time to right a really bad wrong that happened. It was not classified, and nobody ever said it couldn't be discussed. You will see once again how a security report, which I am required to do both by Army regulations, as well as my contractual obligation of deliverable, was covered up to protect the contract, and the mission. The way I see it, go ahead, fire me now. Go ahead and sue me, I don't care. It will bring to the public's attention what happened, and you can't get in trouble if what you are saying is true. I am not an attorney, but I am pretty sure that it's not libel, if it's the truth. Here he is pictured in this photo standing behind Maj. Burris. A simple FOIA request, now that you know what to look for and when, will support everything I claim.

I was the IASO (Information Assurance Security Officer) for the IIA program and responsible for all IT related security on all the computer networks we used. One day, towards the end of the contract, at the same time our contract was up for rebid, I was looking at the event logs for our individual users looking for anomalies that might suggest intrusions or unauthorized activities. I noticed something very strange, one of our staff, an employee of MPRI, the company that was the prime on this contract, had been spending a great deal of time on a website for older men that like to have sex with young, underage boys. This wasn't a one-off thing where someone might accidently click a link that takes you to a site like this and you close right out of it, this guy had a paid membership, and cached his login and password locally on his government issued computer, along with a collection of illicit photos of the most indecent nature that had been cached from his browser. He had been using the "dirty" net, which is the term we use for commercial internet, and not a government network like NIPR. Had he done this on NIPR, he would have likely been busted by another agency that monitors and secures that government network. He had been visiting the site quite regularly. I documented everything in an official report, and took it to our program manager, Russ Hampsey. He is a really good guy by the way and himself a father. Russ was as shocked as I was and immediately reported it to both MPRI corporate, and to Maj. Burris. There was someone else as well from the military I believe, but cannot remember at this time.

Maj. Burris met with both Russ and I and we showed him what I had discovered. As I recall, MPRI had authorized Russ to fire him, and I had been ordered to have him locked out of his network access. When he was confronted with the evidence, he knew he was pretty well done. I was expecting his Top-Secret clearance to be immediately revoked as well, but as you may have learned after reading this far into my book, things don't always work out quite like you would expect.

As I mentioned at the beginning of this chapter, our program was new and was under a great deal of scrutiny. After meeting with Maj. Burris, it was clear that not only would this incident likely have us eliminated from the rebid on this contract, it would likely get the whole operation shut down. Faced with that information, they all asked me how I wanted them to proceed, essentially putting the entire mission and this multi-million dollar contract on me. I told them, and myself, that my job was to report the incident to my chain of command, and ended there. What they did with it was up to them. I know this was the wrong answer, and that I should have pushed this to the IG, but you know what, if I had pushed this, it would have likely come down to me being the one that got in trouble, and everyone else would have protected their own asses.

This is how the system works, and if you keep reading to where I finally lose my job in Korea after having requested whistleblower protection, then you will see that I am absolutely right about how the system works. At that time, in the summer of 2008, there was nothing to protect contractors under the whistleblower protections setup by the IG. As you will read later, even when they did extend contractors the same protections in 2013, I still was not protected.

MPRI did let him go, but I was told he never had his security clearance pulled because it would have triggered an investigation. Our command dropped it to protect the program, and Russ couldn't do anything because he had to answer to MPRI, and they were not about to give up a multi-million dollar contract over something like this. It was wrong on every level. I was wrong, Burris was wrong, and so was Russ and our employers. And in the end, we still ended up losing the contract to a company named Leonie. In fact, Leonie underbid the contract, but wasn't even aware of the fact it required them to provide 2 people for IT, and they only bid based on them providing one – and they still won. I wouldn't be surprised if my reporting it ended up contributing to us being removed, even though nothing was ever done about the pedophile. That's just a guess, mind you, but I wouldn't be surprised if it impacted the military's decision to go with Leonie. The president of my company, Dynology, knew what had happened, as I reported to him on it daily. After our Iraq contract ended, I was given a position back in Tampa supporting a CENTCOM contract. Looking back at it now, after having the gift of hindsight, you can take what happened to me in Korea, and question if I would have had a job back in Tampa, coming back from Iraq, had I pushed it to the IG.

I can say that even with the regrets I have from not pushing this issue, and let's be honest, is it the responsibility of the IT guy once he has taken it to both the program manager and a Major in the Army that was in charge of the program to make these decisions? I will say this again one more time, in the military, the one that usually gets punished, is the one who steps up initially to do the right thing. The key to staying alive, is staying off your employer and client's radar. This incident would have been no different. The only difference is that I was not fired then for reporting it, and was able to go on and work another 7 years before finally being removed for enforcing the rules. After this incident, I felt like such a piece of crap, that I never allowed another person to violate Army regulations without being reported, and when my chain of command didn't do their job, which happened a lot, I continued to push the issues from that point on, with little or any regard to my own personal interests or career.

Leaving Baghdad a Safer Place?

As I mentioned above, we lost the bid to a second year in Iraq. I wasn't planning to stay anyway, and my company, Dynology, had another contract for me to support back in Tampa. The new company that came in was called Leonie, and they had really screwed up when they submitted their bid for this contract. Leonie's new project manager that was coming on board asked both Aaron and I if we wanted to stay, but neither of us did. In a very funny story, we were all standing outside of our office at the sea huts, and the new Leonie program manager was asking Aaron and me if we wanted to stay on and work for them, but for about half the price we were making for the past year. The PM was explaining to us how they would need to cut our salary in half because things were slowing down in Iraq. He said there was less violence, and contracting companies couldn't justify the salary we had been making now that the AQI threat had been reduced. Just as he is saying this, there is a huge explosion just a few hundred meters away from us at a checkpoint on Route Irish. Aaron and I looked at him in disbelief of the timing and I said "yeah, things are clearly much safer here now, but I think we are going to pass on your generous offer." He just stood there with the most dumbfounded look on his face. We then packed up our stuff and headed back to Tampa, where an IIA project like what we had pioneered in Iraq had been picked up by CENTCOM, but on a much larger scale. Little, if anything I did back in Tampa is something that I can discuss outside of just the most generalized terms due to the extreme sensitivity and classification of our deliverables.

On my way back to Tampa I flew into New York, and was in need of a little rest and relaxation. I took the train from NY to

Canada where I met my wife and spent a few weeks at Niagara Falls. We decided to take a romantic train ride back from Canada to Florida and stopped by my company's corporate office in Virginia on the way. It was the first time I had ever been to Dynology's corporate office, and it was really, really, nice. I met the president of Dynology, Jim Jones, in person for the first time and we all had lunch. Jim's father was General James Jones (aka big Jim). Big Jim was a retired 4-star Marine Corp general and former supreme allied commander for NATO.

That evening was the 3rd and last presidential debate between Barak Obama and John McCain. It is relevant to note that Jim and his family were lifelong friends of John McCain. Jim's father, Big Jim, had served with McCain in Vietnam, and Jim's first job was as an intern for McCain years earlier. My wife, Lara, and I were watching the debate the evening before meeting at Dynology, when Obama was asked who his top choice for Secretary of State would be. He suggested General James Jones. I was quite surprised, but not as surprised as either my boss or Big Jim, or so we were told. After Obama won, he tapped Hillary as Secretary of State for what I believe, and knowing the situation as I do, for completely political reasons. I can only imagine how different things would have turned out in Benghazi if Obama had not made a political decision and had stuck with his original idea of James Jones. It's the butterfly effect, like when a small event can make a big difference. But in this situation, the effects from the wings of a butterfly, would be more like a gigantic, winged dragon.

I held the ONLY Obama "Meet-Up" in all of Iraq during the summer of 2008. Because political events were not allowed to be held in a government building, I was forced to hold my Obama Meetup in what I dubbed "The Obama Shelter," which was actually a bomb shelter. I used Photoshop to put "Obama Shelter" on the actual bomb shelter image I used for my flyer. I thought it was a great play on words, and yet another political first for Patrick Bergy! I hope this also serves to dispel any concerns Democrat's reading this book might have about me having some partisan bend towards one political party over the other, especially with the way I have criticized Hillary Clinton.

Prior to the 2000 general presidential election between Bush and Gore, I mostly leaned Democrat. My beef with Bill Clinton was not because he had an affair with someone on his staff, but more because she wasn't as sexy as Marilyn Monroe. I certainly didn't think something like that warranted our government spending $50 million to investigate it, that's for sure.

Worldwide, countries hostile to the U.S. would also be a lot more worried about Hillary, and take her more seriously than they do now if she had, in my personal opinion hacked off Bill's "twig and berries". I also think that once it was clear Bill did in fact have sex with Monica, he should have been responsible for all of the taxpayer dollars spent proving it. I bet if Bill Clinton thought it might personally cost him $50 million in legal fees if he lied about Monica and got caught, he would not have lied. It's a simple rule, really. If you work for the government, lie and get caught, you should have to pay for legal expenses. If the same punishment applied, like what happens in the civilian world, our government employees might choose not to lie as often. There will always be cowards that are afraid to accept the punishment for doing something wrong, and lie about it no matter what the cost. But there would be a lot less of them, and the cowards that do should pay for it, not taxpayers. Anyway, back to the story.

I presented Jim with a flag when we first arrived at the corporate office in Tyson's Corner. It was in a wood and glass case, and the flag had been raised on base in Camp Victory, which he kept on his office wall. It was still there at Dynology's corporate office up to my departure in 2015. We thanked Jim for his support while I was overseas, and headed back to Florida on the next train out. I love trains, and had been away from my wife for about 6 months, so the confined space in our private sleeper car was just the right call ;-) We got back to Tampa and I started in soon after with my new Dynology contract, which was supporting the Joint Military Information Support Command, or JMISC. We called it "Joint Miscellaneous." We were doing much of the same work with un-attributable "dirty" networks, but on a much, much larger scale. Our contract was strictly to develop the network and support the JMISC and their missions. We were involved with the operational aspects, not tactical, and there is not much I can comment that would not violate national security, which I won't do. To be clear, anything I have discussed in my book thus far is all available in bits and pieces online, and nothing I have said violates national security.

It was around January of 2009 and I had been back from Iraq a few months now. Things were good with the family and it was nice to be home. My pool was built and the kids loved it. I had 6 tile sea turtles embedded in the floor of the pool to represent my family, which were everything to me. I had spent now about a year and a half in both Afghanistan and Iraq, and my wife had been home alone taking care of our 4 children. I will not say it was easy on either of us, that is for sure, and I respected all that it took for her to take care of our children all alone, but we began to start dealing with some issues. What we were experiencing as a military family with long deployments, is very common to others in our situation. War had taken a toll on me personally, and I did not return the same person I was before I left.

A year passed and I was told that our contract was not going to be renewed with JMISC, and Dynology did not have another contract to put me on. They had a bid in on a contract in South Korea for a knowledge management officer, but that had not been awarded, and there was no telling if they would win. I put my resume out and got a response from of all companies, Leonie. You may remember them as being the company that took over our contract in Iraq and wanted me to come work for them for about half the money. They had an IIA based program that had just started in Kabul, Afghanistan, and wanted me to join them over there. They were offering a little more than what they had offered me in Iraq, so I discussed it with my wife. Keep in mind now the state of our economy and the employment situation here in the states in 2010 was really bad. With my contract ending with Dynology in a few weeks, we would not be in a good place if I didn't have a job. My wife agreed and supported the decision for me to go back to Afghanistan.

Welcome to Afghanistan - Again

The flight was really long and I was dead tired by the time I arrived at Kabul International Airport – not a military airport, but KIA, the main public airport in Kabul. There I was, surrounded by what looked to be Taliban everywhere, and I probably wasn't too far off with that comment. I was a bit nervous to say the least and wanted to keep a low profile, get through customs, and meetup with my point of contact from Leonie. I had my rucksack and walked down the stairway that was brought to the cabin of our jet. I got to the bottom of the stairs, take my first step back on Afghanistan soil in about two years, trip and fall flat on my face. Yes, in my attempt to stay off the radar and blend in, as much as a 45-year-old white American with blonde hair can blend in. I now had everyone in the airport looking at me. Welcome to Afghanistan Bergy.

I got in the line for customs and had my passport out and ready. The Taliban looking gentlemen ahead of me hands his passport to the official at the passport counter, and I notice it had a large wad of money inside the passport, which was then taken by the Afghan customs agent and placed cleanly into his pocket. Wonderful boarder security here for sure, I'm feeling safer by the minute. In my first trip to Afghanistan with my Army unit we flew directly into a U.S. military base, which I found much more comforting than passing through KIA. I met with my POC from Leonie that appeared to be accustomed with visiting the airport and we drove back to what is known as GV, or Green Village.

GV was much nicer than anyplace I had worked in either Afghanistan or Iraq. It was built by contractors, for contractors, and was guarded by Gurkha's. A serious bunch those Gurkha's, much like when I worked with the Tongan Marines in Iraq, which all looked like Duane "The Rock" Johnson. We were smack dab in the center of Kabul, and pretty much everyone, everywhere looked like they wanted to kill you. We were authorized to carry a weapon when going off base here in Kabul, which made me feel a little better when traveling outside of the fence, which is something we did at least a few times per week. I am 5'11" tall with blonde hair and hazel blue eyes, blending in here was not an option. I got a quick tour and was taken to my quarters. It was nice. I had my own private shower and bath, flat screen television and cable with at least a few English channels. I was supporting an extremely classified project for the Information Operations Task Force Afghanistan (IOTF) and all I can say is that it involved multi-media – that's it. My job was to provide a "dirty" network access to the internet. Anything that could expose us, would immediately put many lives in danger. I was there largely to provide IT security, and make sure nobody outside of our organization could access our network without proper authorization.

I got to work on my first day and was briefed on our mission and shown to my new office. When I started to look around I was shocked at the lack of industry standard hardware for securing the network. Leonie, who are known in the industry for being the lowest bidders, put the lives of our troops and those on our team with the safety of a 5 port Linksys home Wi-Fi router. Everything I was given or authorized was a joke, so I made up a report listing all deficiencies and what we needed to get immediately. I submitted my list to our program manager, and he told me I needed to be more of a team player. I immediately submitted my resignation as shown below.

Operations Manager
Leonie Industries
Camp Green Village
Afghanistan

Dear ████ :

With this letter, I hereby submit my resignation from Leonie Industries, LLC, effective immediately, 02 April, 2010.

I have made my own flight arrangements, departing at16:30 on 03 April, 2010 from Kabul International Airport on KAM Airways. I respectfully request transportation in adequate time to make this flight, so as to avoid any additional expenses to me. Prior to my departure, all Leonie inventories I have signed for will be hand receipted over to you and returned.

That said, the reason for my actions are a direct result of your response to me regarding the network security report I issued to you. I am a Leonie employee, not a sub on this contract. My reason for submitting that report to you was to make you aware of very serious deficiencies in the security and infrastructure of this network. I am a certified Information Assurance Security Officer, and have more than 15 years of IT experience, with the last 9 years focused directly in network security, and the last 5 years directly supporting network infrastructors for the DOD.

It is not in my nature to "stay in my lane and play ball", as you stated. Not when it comes to protecting and maintaining the security of this mission – that is my lane. Drafting a report telling you everything that is right with the network doesn't do anyone any good. The only way I can be of any value is to tell you the truth, and it is up to you as to what you do with it. You made it clear that you do not value either my experience, or the truth, but either way, without that you have no need for me, and there are other missions that can benefit from my knowledge, and there is clearly no place for me here.

I wish only the best for this team and this mission.

I DO NOT nor WILL NOT "stay in my lane" or "play ball" when the lives of our troops or civilian assets are at stake. I have a team, but it's not Team Leonie, or Team Dynology, or Team Engility or Team MPRI. My team is Team America – F*** Yeah!

Literally on my first day in Afghanistan I attended a meeting where Leonie explained to everyone on our team that they had made a few mistakes and were drawing back all assets from outside, to here at GV. This was to make up for their financial losses. In the days that followed I watched requests for even basic network equipment needed to fulfill the requirements of network security, compliance and multimedia production being denied because of insufficient funding. It wasn't always due to funding though. One time a secretary in our human resources department that was doing the ordering, decided to change my request for PC's, to MAC. You see, she had heard more PC's get computer viruses than MAC's, so logically, she changed the order to MAC's. Unfortunately, the software for these systems we needed for our mission was for PC's. Giving a secretary the ability to alter emergency essential equipment being order by a subject matter expert hired to install and setup the network, did not seem to me as the most logical plan. Literally millions were wasted on a poorly planned, financed and executed contract award.

This is an excerpt from an email exchange in 2010 between myself and a senior officer in the U.S. military. It took place just prior to my resigning from the Leonie contract in Afghanistan, 2010. I just though it perfectly describes the corrupt relationship between our military and the military industrial complex (the swamp) for which I am sharing with you now in my book. I have removed his name and identifiable information to protect his identity.

From: Patrick Bergy
"(Name Removed), what is my responsibility as a network admin that, if (hypothetically, of course) I did see things being so jacked up that I was to consider resigning, what is my responsibility to the command. Would I just put my reasons down in writing to my employer and leave, or do I bring this to the attention of my command as well. I struggle with this, and ask for your guidance as a friend.
You remember that in the past when I did try to bring these things up to my incoming commander, it fell on deaf ears, which has sort of made me question what to do now, hypothetically speaking, of course..."

The incident I reported but "fell on deaf ears" as mentioned above, pertained to the contractor with a Top-Secret clearance in Iraq. He was the pedophile I filed an official security report on for downloading horrific acts of pornography involving older men having sex with underage boys. Ironically, we lost the contract anyway to Leoni a few days later. I cannot even imagine what they did to all the work I had pioneered in Interactive Internet Activities in Iraq after they took over, but if what I saw in Afghanistan was any indication, it was not very good.

This was the officer's response to my question in the email shown above:

> *"Now, to the root of your question--you have no obligation to the command. Your obligation is to the site manager/contract manager. Since we are speaking hypothetically, I hate the way the Army manages its contracts most of the time. We constrain ourselves to the point of letting the contractor have all the power and that is the fault of the military. What made the IIA so successful when we were in Iraq was the fact that we all worked TOGETHER. Sure, we had some personality issues and that happens when a bunch of guys are stuck together--it's pretty much inevitable but when the military just gives in to the contractor and sticks its head in the sand, real problems arise. My advice to you (not knowing the problems--and if you are indeed working the contract that I will fall in on, please don't tell me what they are because I will be there soon enough) is to fulfill the terms of your contract for now. Once you have completed what you signed up to do and if things are still crap, just move on from there. As you know, in the contracting world your reputation is basically your paycheck so I'd just hang in there a few more weeks and change is on the horizon.*

It pretty much says it all, doesn't it? The system is so absolutely broken, words cannot describe it with any justice. The only way you will ever end the corruption in military contracting, is to end military contracting. Sure, you will then have to deal with corruption in our government and military, but it is a lot easy to deal with one, that it is to deal with them both. I discuss this in much more detail, and provide a unique solution in the conclusion of the book.

5   Korea – The Good Side

In less than two days after resigning from the contract in Afghanistan with Leonie, on April 4th 2010, I arrived in Seoul, South Korea, to begin my contract with Dynology and the United States Forces Korea (UFSK) in support of USFK J8 Transformation and Relocation. It was not as high speed as IIA, and didn't pay as well as in Iraq or Afghanistan, but one thing it did do, was allow my family to come and live here with me in Korea in a gorgeous high-rise apartment in the center of Seoul. Oh, and there was a lot less likelihood of someone trying to kill you with a mortar round or suicide bomb. That was a good thing also.

Having come from working in actual war zones where people work together and the mission comes first, Korea was a big shock to the system. Most U.S. government employees I worked with and met, have never seen any type of combat. This largely applies to the military stationed there as well. The level of dysfunction was unimaginable. I like to compare the U.S. government employees in South Korea, with the Vogan's, from the book "A Hitchhiker's Guide to the Galaxy." It's as if everyone working there came from a planet where individual thought was rewarded with a sharp smack to the forehead. The paperwork required for pretty much anything is ridiculous as well. To get permission to ride my Segway, which I purchased stateside and shipped here, I had to threaten a 15-year division director and government bureaucrat with violating the disabilities act, as I had gotten herniated disc while in a combat zone, and have a line of duty to prove it. My request was initially denied because a $6,000 Segway looks a lot like an electric skateboard, and electric skateboards are not authorized on base. This was the actual words that come from the director's mouth. You cannot use a logical argument, like Segway's are allowed on most U.S. military bases, and Army regulations and guidelines have already been set for its use on base. But, threaten a career politician or government employee with violating the rights of a disabled Afghanistan veteran, and they will kiss your butt. I may have left out that my line of duty was from lifting cases of Gatorade.

I need to take a moment at this point in my story to tell you about when I first arrived at USAG Yongsan in South Korea, and what happened a few days ago as I was working on this book. I woke on 06/11/2016 to yet another act of terrorism on American soil. The attack in Orlando was the worst single act of terror by an active shooter in America's history. As information surrounding the attack started coming out, I heard that the attacker, Omar Mateen, was an employee of a company called G4S. To make matters worse, it came out that at least one of his co-workers at G4S had quit, after complaints he had made surrounding the actions of the would-be Orlando shooter, were reportedly ignored by G4S. Why is this relevant to this point in my book? Because when I arrived on base at USAG Yongsan in South Korea on a military contract in 2010, I was greeted at the gates of the base by U.S. and Korean Soldiers, supported by a Korean contracting company. There were around 11 gates, most of which were all manned during common business hours, which was nice because when a gate is closed on a base the size of USAG Yongsan, it could take a long time to drive around to the next open gate. About a year later, this all changed when the contract to provide gate security at USAG Yongsan was awarded to G4S. Yes, you guessed it right, the low bidder. The decision to award the contract to G4S not only ended up with about 400 Koreans that were trained, experienced, and paid a living wage losing their jobs, they were protesting by the hundreds because of the meager wages offered by G4S. They closed 6 of the 11 gates to the base, which was a nightmare that likely resulted in significant loss of productivity on base, and security was significantly impacted. I don't know the actual reason, but if it had anything to do with what I saw in Iraq and Afghanistan contracts, many companies get the lowest bids, but end up lacking the staff and resources to fulfill the contract. I think much of this problem stems from the cost a company has in even presenting a proposal. I know companies that have spent a million dollars just to prepare a proposal, and lose the bid. Companies end up cutting overhead with the proposal process, and just copy and paste the requirements from the RFP, or request for proposal. This is a shame, as many companies actually bid based on the actual deliverables, and lose to companies that, for example, base their bid on providing 12 hours a day support for a 24-hour contract deliverable. Clearly, in many cases they don't fully understand the deliverables, bid low and figure it out with the government afterwards. They either go back and ask for more money in a "cost plus" contract, or just provide 12 hours of support. You will read of several examples of this in my book. As for the Orlando active shooter, you will understand why I am not surprised to hear the incident reports were ignored by G4S. When you read of my experience over the last decade I have spent in support of our military, I truly hope you can begin to feel my pain as an American Patriot. Having personally witnessed how G4S handled the contract in South Korea, I am clearly not a big fan of them. Additionally, I make no claim to knowing what happened with G4S and the Orlando shooter. That said, the initial reports from G4S co-workers sounds exactly as I have experienced and described having happened to me in my book. You will really see this in the coming chapters with even more clarity. Protect the client and protect the contract at all cost. But what is the cost? Were the lives of about 50 victims in the Orlando shooting part of the cost of the reports that were ignored by G4S? Was any part of their decision made to protect their contract? Will the next cost be the lives of our troops in Korea because we chose the lowest bidder, instead of just having enough of our own troops stationed on base to provide for its own security? Please think about this question as you read my book, and ask yourself if when the next act of terror happens, was there really nothing that we could have done different?

On my first day in South Korea (that's the good side) I was greeted with some paperwork that was required to be filled out and submitted to contracting. Once contracting was complete, they would issue you what is called a form 700-19, which you could then take and get your SOFA (Status of Forces Agreement) visa. When they saw that I had come from Afghanistan, contracting sent back a request for me to prove that I had not lived in Afghanistan with the intent of becoming a citizen of Afghanistan. A utility bill from the states would do. Seriously, this was really a thing. In 2013 this guy Justin came here after working on a contract in Iraq for 3 years. He didn't have a utility bill from the states, and it took him nearly a month to get his 700-19. In fact, most everyone that arrives in Korea will wait about 3-4 weeks before they get their 700-19. Unfortunately, you cannot shop at the PX, get your SOFA stamp, or get a CAC card which allows you access on base during that time, or access to the military networks you are required to access for your job. Yes, for 3 weeks those that did not come here with a CAC, or have a retiree card from the military need to be escorted on base to work – every day. In 2012, we had a "surge" team of about 15 folks the government paid a lot of money for as subject matter experts to work on a special project. The contract was for 3 months, and nearly every single one of them waited nearly 30 days to get their 700-19's. That meant they could only access the USFK portal, where all the documents they needed to work on are kept, for almost 1/3 of the time they were hired to be here. Tell me that is not waste and abuse?

As for me I was able to get my 700-19 in just a few days, and I have no idea how that happened. Getting my admin CAC that allowed me to do the work I came here to do, took about 45 days, but there was still a lot I could do without my admin CAC, so for me, it wasn't that big of a deal. What in the world could possibly take that long for something as basic and essential as being able to begin doing the work you were hired by the U.S. government to do, or even to shop on base, or use the U.S. Post Office on base?

Everyone I mentioned has at least a secret level clearance. Who in their right mind would think that I, spending 2 months in Afghanistan, working for the U.S. military with a Top-Secret clearance, could possibly have been considering citizenship in Afghanistan? But aside from the overwhelming bureaucracy, South Korea was a beautiful place, and I was so excited to have my family moving here to stay with me on what was at that time a three-year contract. That is when things started to go terribly, terribly wrong in my 1st marriage.

The excitement of the family moving to South Korea ended a few months later when my wife filed for divorce. I can only say that likely my years of deployments had taken too much of a toll on our marriage, and likely a splash of PTSD thrown in there for good measure. Out of consideration to my first wife and my children, I will not discuss this in other than general terms. I can say that I never cheated on her, or did anything personally wrong, it's just things got broken in our marriage that we were not able to fix. I struggle deeply with many regrets surrounding how I handled the situation to this day. Like I stated in this books dedication, I hope someday the two years I spent writing this book will help my children to better understand. I am not shooting for father of the year, but none of us know how long we have left in our life, and if I were to die tomorrow, what would my children tell their kids about their grandfather?

USFK J8

Through all the absolute chaos that has taken place in my life since arriving in Korea with my divorce, I still performed exceptionally in my work. I was building out a new SharePoint site for USFK J8 which enhances collaboration of our members in J8 with documents and such. A taxonomy is sort of like a standard you develop for keywords that helps make it easier to collaborate and find things on a computer. I developed for J8's SharePoint site the taxonomy from scratch, and I did it based on using an existing Army document called the 10-1, aka, the Organizations and Functions manual. This had never been thought of before, at least that was what I was told by the USFK Knowledge Management folks. It was actually the perfect document to use to build a taxonomy with. A taxonomy is used to create those drop down lists you use when filling out a form online, for example. Sometimes you enter words manually, like your name because it is something unique. But when you put in your zip code and the city field automatically populates, that is because of a zip code taxonomy built into the application. There are several ways people can spell the name of a city. People that live in St. Petersburg, Fl., might spell it out, like Saint

Petersburg, and some might spell it as St. Pete. When you are creating a document library with literally millions of documents, you want as many of your search fields to be spelled the same say, so if I am searching for something from Saint Petersburg, I know all the documents from that area will be included, and not leave out the one's spelled "St. Pete." The 10-1 is a manual the Army has used for years, and describes the exact name of each organization and its specific function. So, by coming up with the idea to use a document that already existed, is updated annually, and was the same for everyone, it was perfect for building not only J8's taxonomy, but for the entire Korean peninsula. About a year earlier, USFK put out a contract that brought in a company to develop a taxonomy for USFK. If I am not mistaken, this contract cost about $500,000. To my knowledge, the work on the convoluted taxonomy they did make, but never completed, was never implemented. Who knows how much that wasted taxpayer dollars? So, hey, using the Organization and Functions manual was something we already had, and didn't require hiring an outside company to develop one. It was the perfect solution, but wait, we're in Korea and you haven't forgotten how dysfunctional things are out here have you?

Totally Preventable, Catastrophic Loss of Data

The issue surrounding Hillary Clinton and her use of a private email server, is a very personal issue to me. Hillary Clinton, in my opinion, has never honestly answered her true reason for using a private email server. I believe her true reason behind using a private email server was to allow her privacy. I respect the fact that most of her life she has had every moment scrutinized by the press, and her opponents, and so has Donald Trump, and I don't think it is right.

Even the most basic examination of my life would make me appear as someone I truly am not, but that is beside the point. She let her authority get in the way of what is in the best interest of national security. Such abuse of authority is the rule in our government, not the exception, but this cannot be used to excuse her behavior. This book is my last shot at having someone held accountable for what you will read next. Change will only come when our leaders begin to lead by example, and not use it to their personal benefit.

USFK J8 consists of 4 divisions. J80, J82, J83, and J84. When I came on board in 2010, the J8 Director was SES Rich Parker. He is an exception to the rule when it comes to leadership in the government. He is exceptionally intelligent and was a great director. His deputy was Regina Adams, and in mid-2012 she tasked both myself and Randy Olsen, a GS employee, with migrating all of J8's data for the last several years. We were moving millions of government documents from a single physical server in our office, to a virtual server that was highly redundant, and protected the data from loss or theft. I quickly completed all the required paperwork, but it needed to be signed by a 06 or above, and submitted by a GS employee or military. Contractors are not allowed to authorize such funding. I sent the completed paperwork to Randy, a GS government employee working with J83, on several occasions. He never took that final step of getting the required government signatures and submitting the official request. All of our data remained at risk on this one physical server in our office for over a year waiting on these signatures. Remember, the deputy director tasked us to do this, and the deputy had put off tasking it for nearly a year from the time USFK command, a 3-star general required the migration. Regina, our J8 deputy, in an email to me, claimed she didn't want to give up physical control of J8's data, much like Hillary didn't like giving up control of hers. From an IT security perspective, this was the safest and most secure action we could be taking, and I sent her reminders of the USFK requirement to migrate the data several times during that first year.

Then one day in October 2013, we got a new division chief in J83. His name was COL McFadden. He requested a meeting to be briefed on the state of our SharePoint portal, and to know what the status was on our data, and if it was being properly backed up. The briefing was a disaster, as he had not wanted me to explain what J8 was doing with SharePoint. What he really wanted was to tell me what he wanted, and how he wanted it done. The problem with that is I answer to the J8 director, Rich Parker, and so does he.

Rich Parker had participated in the development of the new SharePoint portal, and signed off on all the work I had done over the last year in developing the new portal and taxonomy. The lower J8 sub-divisions, including J83, were expected to follow his instructions. I professionally and respectfully explained to the COL that I would be more than happy to implement his suggestions, but that I would need to take his request to SES Parker first. He became furious, and cut short my prepared briefing.

After cutting short the briefing, the COL asked for myself, two other contractors in attendance, and Randy Olsen to sit down and answer a few questions. One of the questions was on the state of our data and how it was backed up. I answered him honestly, and took the opportunity to explain that we, (Randy Olsen and I) had been ordered by the J8 deputy to migrate the data to USFK's virtual servers over a year ago. I explained to him I had all the required paperwork completed and submitted to Randy nearly a year ago, but needed Randy to get it signed off by an authorized government employee, as contractors were not allowed to do this. I explained I have been trying to get this done for over a year with no success, and asked him, right in front of Randy, if he could help to make this happen. The COL then instructed Randy to get right on it. Instead of getting right on it, Randy drafted an email to my program manager (my in-country boss) saying that I had thrown him under the bus, and that he was very upset and wanted me taken off from supporting J83's knowledge management.

I had already submitted a detailed after-action report to my program manager that told of how the meeting went, and that I had informed them of this very serious issue that jeopardized all of J8's data. I also noted in my official report, that I was hopeful at least one good thing was going to come from this meeting, in that we were finally going to have our data migrated.

Our program manager, Buck Buchanan, whom worked for MPRI, called me into his office to discuss the email he had received from Randy. Buck explained to me that although I did nothing wrong, he was going to be taking me off support for J82 and J83, and placing the new guy, Justin Losh, with MPRI as their support. So instead of something good coming from this, I was punished and removed from over 80% of my responsibilities. Justin, who was new and hadn't even gotten his 700-19 authorized yet, and could not even access the network, was now in charge of J82 and J83. Justin's primary responsibilities were already to support the J4, which was another division with nearly 300 users, several times larger than J8, and there was no way he could provide any type of responsible support to J82 and J83 deliverables, but that is what happened.

About 3 weeks later I came in and found that lightening had taken out a switch in our office. The Area 2 NEC, which provides IT hardware support for all USFK, had been tasked with updating the software on our physical server that same week. When the A2NEC remoted into our server, which was located at J8 headquarters just across the street from my office and tried to update it, the whole system failed, and all the data was now lost. Yes, three weeks after warning our command that our data was in jeopardy and we needed to act, but was then removed from supporting them because I had upset a GS employee, was now lost.

It was more important to punish me for doing my job, than migrating the data. It was now all lost on a failed and damaged hard drive, and would have to be sent out to a private company at great expense to see if any of the data was even recoverable. I was furious after having been punished for warning them about this very risk, instead of fixing the problem. Worse yet, everyone in J8 now blamed me for the loss of all their data, and our program manager had locked me down and prohibited me from sending any emails to anyone without his reading it first and approving it. He wanted to control the situation and not upset the client by getting them in trouble for retaliating against me after I had filed an official report. My official report clearly shows this massive, catastrophic loss of data was preventable.

To add insult to injury, Randy Olsen, who was largely responsible for the data loss, in my opinion, was the one tasked with getting the data recovered, and finally migrating to USFK's virtual servers where all new data would be properly secured and backed up. It is of significance to note that our contract for the next option year is renewed, or "optioned" every year around this time, and the last thing MPRI wanted was for me to be making waves. All I wanted to do was my job. Additionally, at this point my report clearly shows Col McFadden was also responsible for the loss of data, and we were heading for a huge change-up in our command.

This change in our leadership would soon place Col McFadden with absolute power throughout all USFK J8. It is simply remarkable to me how this much power ended up in the hands of just one man. The system is setup to prevent this. I can only imagine having one person with absolute authority over a $10 billion-dollar budget is kind of why they set the system up to prevent it in the first place.

Not only did Buck, our program manager, not push to get an investigation into this tremendous loss of data, he intentionally, and I believe illegally modified emails to cover the incident up and keep the blame on me. A few days after the data loss, Buck received an email request from our command asking for the documentation required for getting the virtual servers brought online. When Buck asked me for the documentation, I forwarded him the original email I sent Randy Olsen back in February, a full 8 months before we lost the data in

Moses,
This is the documentation needed to submit for the RD. Let Patrick and Justin know when is a good time to meet if J8 decides to ask for back up space. They can help in document preparation.

Buck
Lloyd W. Buchanan, Jr. - CTR
Engility USFK Consolidated Transformation Team
Program Manager
DSN:
Cell:

Header intentionally removed

Randy:

This is the documentation we need to submit for the RD. Let me know when is a good time to meet with you so we can complete correctly together.

Patrick

Patrick B. Bergy (Contractor)
Dynology Corporation
IT/KM Administrator
Transformation and Force Development USFK J8
DSN:
KOR-

-----Original Message-----
From: Weston, Michael CIV USARMY 1 SIG BDE (US)
Sent: Wednesday, April 10, 2013 8:15
To: Bergy, Patrick B CTR USARMY USFK (US)
Cc: kim, maurice M CIV USARMY 1 SIG BDE (US); Im, Jin S CIV USARMY 1 SIG

Header not removed

October. This was one of a half-dozen times I had gone to Randy and reminded him we had been tasked by the J8 deputy, to migrate our physical server to the new VM. I forwarded Buck the email with the required documents that showed the header information in the email as being from February. I explained to Buck that this would be a good opportunity to let our command know that this data loss was entirely preventable, and that Patrick had spent over a year trying to prevent it by having Randy complete the required paperwork. Buck gets my email, reads my comments about taking this opportunity to show J8 command what had happened, and then removes the header information before forwarding the email to our XO. He left all other header information from the original thread, removing only the date Randy Olsen had originally received the email. The original email I had forwarded Buck specifically informed him that the header information would be a great way to clear my name in all of this, and he intentionally removes it.

Several months later, in February, 2014, I send Buck an email asking him if there has been any investigation into the massive loss of data, reminding him that I believed such an investigation was actually required by DoD regulations, and that he should take the opportunity he had in a meeting he was to be attending to remind J8 command of this requirement.

Nearly a month later, in March of 2014, Buck sends me a reply to clarify what I meant about issue #4 in the attached file.

Tue 3/25/2014 2:38 AM

Buchanan, Lloyd Wayne (Buck) Jr CTR USARMY USFK (US)

FW: J83 KM Way Ahead (UNCLASSIFIED)

To   Bergy, Patrick B CTR USARMY USFK (US)

Signed By   There are problems with the signature. Click the signature button for details.

🛈 You forwarded this message on 10/27/2015 8:30 AM.

Message   📄 J83 Knowledge Management v1.docx

Patrick,
As I prepare for the Friday meeting, it brings me back to your email. You make mention of Note #4 in the AAR. Help me to find note #4 in your AAR as I can only see up to three.
Buck

Within 9 minutes of my response reminding him of how nothing has been done to investigate potentially millions of dollars in data loss, which was completely preventable, Buck responds that all emails are to go through him first for review before being sent to anyone in J8 leadership.

Tue 3/25/2014 2:47 AM

Buchanan, Lloyd Wayne (Buck) Jr CTR USARMY USFK (US)
KM/SharePoint Work

To   Bergy, Patrick B CTR USARMY USFK (US); Losh, Justin M CTR USARMY USFK (US)

Signed By   There are problems with the signature. Click the signature button for details.

ⓘ You forwarded this message on 10/27/2015 8:41 AM.

As we embark on a yet to be announced path for J8 KM/SharePoint, which may or may not impact on the J4, please ensure I am copied on all emails related to your work on this contract.

Buck

We don't want Bergy rocking the boat with some misplaced desire to ensure Army regulations are followed. This is how things are done. Don't do anything that could potentially cause problems for the client and jeopardize the renewal of our option years on this multi-million-dollar contract.

Instead of taking multiple opportunities to do the right thing, like maybe follow DoD regulations and requirements, and here's an idea, clear the name of Patrick Bergy, the contractor whom from the beginning was the only one speaking out trying to prevent the eventual loss of all J8's data. The evidence of misconduct by the prime contracting company is overwhelmingly clear. Altering emails is clearly fraud, and instructing subs on the contract to not go around him under any circumstances, is an abuse of his authority. He is in the position to do the right thing, but is not going to do anything to upset the client or follow the guidelines from the Department of Defense. The regulations are designed to hold those responsible accountable, and to help prevent such incidents from happening in the future.

It all goes back to what that officer I worked with in Iraq said to me in his email about the relationship between contractors and the military regarding the incident with the pedophile. Contractors don't want to lose their multi-million-dollar contracts, and the military doesn't want to hurt their relationships with these large corporations because they want to work for them after they leave. We aren't looking for the cure to cancer here. The root of the cause is clear in this situation, and the symptoms are easy to treat. Everything relating to rules and regulations meant to protect our troops and national security comes in dead last, and what is best for them personally, is what is most important. I don't ever see this changing. It is just simple fraud, waste, and abuse in the swamp like relationship between the government and the military industrial complex.

All of this was really starting to come back on me hard in the form of retaliation. Removing me from my area of responsibility, taking away my duties and monitoring my every email to ensure I am "playing ball" as these folks like to say. But I am not playing ball, I am very carefully trying to balance not losing my job, which is how I support my children, and not letting people get away with circumventing the rules and corrupting the system. It was clear that if I made one wrong move, I am done. I continued to document everything and remain patient.

A few months went by and it was now around January 2014. Nothing had been done yet to recover the data or getting the virtual servers online for the new data that J8 was producing. I had sent a few emails reminding my program manager that nothing was being done, but he just said it was the government's responsibility and to stay in my lane. Of course, what I'm thinking was that this was my lane, but you removed me instead of acting on my recommendations, which is how this all happened in the first place. I also sent several emails requesting an investigation into the loss of the data. This is required when there is a data breach or loss of this size to hold those responsible and to help prevent it from happening again in the future. There are also Federal regulations that were violated which require retention of all emails and other products. If that sounds familiar, this is one of the key violations the FBI was considering with Hillary's private email server.

Meanwhile, all the work I had been doing on the portal, and with the development of the taxonomy had been put on hold. I was stuck sitting in my office with nothing to do but watching movies and getting paid. That might sound like a good thing, but I really liked what I had done with the portal and wanted to get it going.

SES Parker was moving on about this time, and he was being replaced by COL McFadden, who absolutely hated me since the first briefing. MPRI, the prime on the contract, had completely isolated me from the government to protect their multi-million-dollar contract, and I knew the moment I heard he was being replace by the COL, things were only going to get worse for me.

The PII Incident – Email Security Matters

In February 2014, I received an email from a GS employee in J82, Dwight Patton. I had worked with Dwight four years now and I like him, but he, just like many of the others, seemingly blamed me for the data loss and all the trouble it had caused them. It is hard to understand the full cost of the loss of all this data, but this might help to put it somewhat in perspective. J84 was the USFK Comptroller's office, and they lost almost everything. Think about what I just said. Everything the military, government, and contract support in J8, J82, J83 and J84 had done was now lost. This required them to either re-create the product (documents) wherever possible from scratch, or piecing it back together from old emails and such. I calculated the loss in man hours of work at around one million dollars by the time what data could be recovered was recovered nearly 9 months later. The damage to me professionally was tremendous, but as a patriot and someone that really believed what they did mattered, it was an even deeper feeling of loss for me mentally. Again, all of what was lost had been completely avoidable.

Dwight had sent an email to Buck, our program manager, but I was included in the email accidentally. The email was sent unencrypted and contained the names and social security numbers of pretty much all J8 contract support. Dwight even noted in his original email that he was sending what we call PII, or personally identifiable information. He then explained he had to send it unencrypted, because he had a problem blacking out social security numbers and such. So, he knew by his own written admission what he was doing was wrong, but sent it anyway.

I throw out a quick comparison of what Dwight did that seems to me as very similar to what Hillary Clinton did in her e-mail scandal in the next chapter. It is from my perspective as a former

Information Assurance Security Officer with the Department of Defense, and I have not yet heard it in the news reporting of Hillary's private email server. But back to the story.

So, I responded back to both Dwight and Buck informing them that this was a PII security violation, and they needed to delete the files and have the J8 security officer (Randy Olsen) make an incident report. The following day I received an email response from Buck that told me I should have gone to him first before sending that. He stated I only did it to cause trouble, and that if I didn't stop making waves, he was going to have me fired. By this point I am really getting pissed. Nowhere in AR 25-1 (Army Regulations manual) does it say in the event of a PII security event like this, that I am supposed to contact my program manager first. I actually did exactly what is required of everyone in this situation. Furthermore, I didn't want to get Dwight in trouble, I liked Dwight and it really wasn't that big of a deal what he had done. His punishment would have at best resulted in a warning from our command, and him being required to take the 10-question IA test again. Retesting was probably a good idea because what he did was wrong, and he acknowledged it before he sent it. What was wrong in all of this was Buck threatening to fire me for reporting a security violation. Don't forget, at this point I was still being punished for my data loss report about 6 months earlier, and was still not allowed to provide support for J82, the division where Dwight worked. Perhaps if I had been providing support, Dwight would have contacted me to help him encrypt the PII, which was literally the work I was contracted and being paid to do by the U.S. government.

So that night I forwarded Buck's email threatening to have me replaced to my employer, Dynology. In it I detailed not just about being told I was going to be fired for reporting a security breach, but I also told them how I had been removed from all my responsibilities several months ago for the data loss incident, and that I have been retaliated against ever since by having virtually all of my responsibilities taken away. Dynology agreed that what I did was appropriate, and was going to have our HR person contact Buck. 2 days later my responsibilities were restored for supporting J82 and J83, and Buck sent out an email (captured below,) to all contractors informing them of the PII incident.

All,

I am writing to you because of a recent accidental security spillage incident within J8. I received an email with an attachment that had all our SSN's listed on a document. The attachment was sent in error and was not intentional. The sender was notified and I deleted the email from my inbox and then emptied my Deleted Items. The other person on the email did the same. I subsequently reported this spillage to the Contract Officer, COR, J8 Security Officers and the Director J8.

While I think the risk is very low, more likely extremely low that the PII was compromised to anyone other than the three of us, to ensure that extra margin of protection, you may wish to consider placing fraud alert on your credit cards. A fraud alert lets creditors know to contact you before opening new accounts. Just call any one of the three credit reporting agencies at the number below. This will let you automatically place fraud alerts with all of the agencies. You will then receive letters from all of them, with instructions on how to get a free copy of your credit report from each.

Equifax	Experian	TransUnion
1-800-525-6285	1-888-397-3742	1-800-680-7289

To protect yourself further from the possibility of identity theft, you may wish to complete a Federal Trade Commission ID Threat Affidavit. This will allow you to legally notify your creditors that your identity may have been compromised. Any debts incurred after that date will not be assigned to you.

Finally, I recommend that you look your credit reports over carefully when you receive them. Look for accounts you did not open. Look for inquiries from creditors that you did not initiate. And look for personally identifiable information, such as home address or Social Security Number that is not accurate. If you see anything you do not understand, call the credit reporting agency at the telephone number on your report. If you do find suspicious activity on your credit reports, call your local police or sheriff's office and file a police report of identity theft. [Or, if appropriate, give contact number for law enforcement agency investigating the incident.] Get a copy of the police report. You may need to give copies of the police report to creditors to clear up your records. Even if you do not find any signs of fraud on your reports, you should check your credit report every three months for the next year. Just call one of the numbers above to order your reports and keep the fraud alert in place. For more information on identity theft, suggest that you visit the Identity Theft Website of the Federal Trade Commission.

http://www.consumer.ftc.gov/features/feature-0014-identity-theft

Sorry for being the bearer of bad news about this PII spillage, but am required to inform so you can take steps for further protection.

Sincerely, Buck

The above screen capture of the email Buck sent out to everyone is what should have happened to begin with, not threatening to fire me for following procedure and reporting it. I do take some issue with Buck saying this was an accident and not intentional, as Dwight actually stated in the original email that he was aware it was PII, and instead of contacting me to help him encrypt it properly, he just sent it out knowing it was wrong. Again, lets protect the client that was clearly in the wrong, and threaten the guy contracted to protect national security with termination. I would also add that you can't just pick up your DSN phone on base in Korea and dial an 800-number stateside, it is quite involved. I doubt anyone took this with the seriousness it deserved, and MPRI's response, in my personal and professional opinion, was pitiful.

The USFK J8 Coup D'état

By this point things were not looking good for me. The J8 director, SES Parker, had left. COL McFadden was put in charge of all J8 until they could find a replacement. It all started a few months earlier, when the J8 deputy director, Regina Adams, had left, and COL. McFadden, the J83 Chief, was made acting deputy director as well.

The J84 chief, COL Kent, was originally named as the interim J8 deputy, but had been forced to leave under very quit and suspicious circumstances. He simply relieved of his command. COL McFadden was then put in charge as the J84 chief, and because he had no replacement for his old position as the J83 chief, COL McFadden was also the acting J83 chief.

So, just to quickly recap… The guy that absolutely hates me for questioning his authority, and in my opinion partially responsible for the data loss, was now the acting J8 director, J8 deputy director, J83 chief and J84 (Comptroller) chief. Even more frightening, essentially one man was now in charge of finances for the entire transformation and relocation of all 8th Army in Korea, to the new base being built called Camp Humphries, and a budget somewhere in the ballpark of $10 BILLION DOLLARS!

I believe the transformation and relocation to Camp Humphries is one of the largest, if not the largest, in our military's history.

A replacement finally came in to replace COL McFadden as the J83 chief, and McFadden immediately tasked the new GS guy that replaced him, Dr. James Knowles, as being in charge of J8 knowledge management. Having had just a few weeks earlier my contract support responsibilities restored for all of J8, I was contacted by Dr. Knowles to have administrative permissions assigned to him on the USFK domain and J8 SharePoint portal. He wanted this done for both unclassified (NIPR) and Secret (SIPR) networks. He emailed me a request for escalated privileges and administrative rights, and I emailed him back with the required documents. A memo signed by an O6 or above as well as several certifications were required to have these rights. This is not my rule, it is a DISA regulation. He responds back to me with a scathing phone call in which he is shouting at me and threatening me to just do it. I told him that I couldn't, and that he needed to complete the paperwork and I would submit it to USFK, because they are the ones that assign and authorize the permissions he requested – not me.

The next day Dr. Knowles called a meeting and told myself and Buck Buchanan that he and McFadden had decided nothing is to be done to the portals without their permission. Additionally, all of the work I had done for over a year for SES Parker, which had already been authorized by director Parker, was not going to be implemented. We were going to be doing things their way for now on. He told both myself and my program manager, Buck Buchanan, I was to stand fast and not do anything until instructed otherwise. Buck later reminds Dr. Knowles in an email about a year later, in April 2015, of our standing order not to do anything without his specific guidance. I have this email.

That was in April of 2014, and I waited until April 2015, doing virtually nothing but coming into work and watching movies I downloaded online and brought in on my personal laptop. There were a few things he tasked me with during that years' time, but they were mostly in direct violation of network security protocols and Army regulations. I emailed my program manager back when he did this, and said what he was asking could result in the loss of my clearance. I told him that they would have to fire me before I would do it, and with hindsight being 20/20, I should have reported the violations then to the IG. Each time I did document the incidents and reported it to my chain of command, which was MPRI, but they did nothing with my incident reports. Other than these handful of unlawful tasks I refused to do, I had nothing to do for an entire year.

Largely founded out of boredom, I set out on a personal mission to fix the problem with accessing U.S. TV shows while deployed overseas. You will read about my personal experience detailed in the "MOPS Networks – Free VOD to Our Troops!" chapter. However, before this I want to make the point of how common most of the things that happened to me as a contractor really is. Again, I see this abuse of authority as consistently being more the rule, than the exception. I am basing the following examples from the point of view as a subject matter expert with nearly 10 years with the Department of Defense as an Information Assurance Security Officer (IASO,) and not political partisanship.

MOPS Networks – Free VOD To Our Troops!

Knowing my days in the contracting business and in J8 were numbered, I used the last year to setup a veteran based non-profit company called MOPS Networks. One thing that triggered this was having lost my ability to watch the Daily Show and Colbert Report online. On a side note, I'm so disgusted with how they both now attack President Trump, I can't even watch either.

With new geo-location filters put in place by Comedy Central and ISP's, I found this to be the last straw, and something needed to be done. People serving our nation overseas should have the right to access programs back home, and everyday increasingly more of the limited number of shows we had been able to watch, were being taken away from us, and I was not going take it anymore. With all the free time I had on my hands, I set out with some colleagues and a personal friend whom was a 3-time Purple Heart recipient, to put together a non-profit organization that would provide a way for our troops overseas to access U.S. themed content.

Shortly after we started to put things together, I saw on AFN a report that they (AFN) had submitted a sources-sought request to determine possible options for providing video on demand to our overseas military. Their fbo.gov sources sought had two different options.

Option #1 would have a potential vendor provide the content, license it to AFN and provide the streaming services.

Option #2 was for AFN to provide the licensed content to a vendor that would provide the streaming services.

As a non-profit I thought this would be a perfect solution. If AFN would provide us their licensed content, as they described in option #2, we could, as a non-profit, provide the streaming services, and our general public supporters could fund much of the streaming in the form of a tax-deductible donation. I presented the idea in an email to the director of television for AFN, and he replied with what amounted to a really sort of rude response. He indicated AFN could not provide a third-party vendor content under their licensing. I found his response to be strange because their sources sought listed that very scenario as an option. It didn't sound right, so I asked for an explanation, but didn't get a response.

We dropped the idea and registered our veteran based non-profit to attend NATPE (National Association of Television Producers and Executives). It was being held February, 2015, in Miami.

The NATPE convention went well and we made several great connections with MGM, FOX, Disney and others. All were very interested in speaking with us further about licensing content that could be made available to our troops overseas through our veteran based non-profit. Several of them we met with currently donated licensed content to AFN, but were not eligible for any tax deductions with their contribution of content to our troops serving overseas. Many companies donate content to our troops through AFN, but as AFN is <u>NOT</u> a non-profit, these companies don't get a tax deduction for the content they contribute. Most of the executives we met with agreed in our meetings at NATPE this was a great idea. Most of the corporations, like FOX Entertainment, have some very lucrative financial agreements with some of the content they provide through AFN as well.

We were curious what they thought about the idea of donating content to MOPS, which would not only provide our troops overseas with much better access to content via the internet and video on demand, but also provide these companies with a potential tax deduction in the process. Again, without exception, the response we received was great with most every executive we met at NATPE.

The AFN / FOX Entertainment Scandal

A few weeks after NATPE I was following up with some of the people we met, and many were not taking my calls. I couldn't understand why, until one day I contacted FOX Entertainment, and what follows is what I claimed in my publicly available report to the Defense Media Activities (DMA's) Inspector General. I called FOX entertainment and the lady that answered the phone became very rude to me the moment I identified myself to her. I didn't understand why, and this was the first time I had spoken to her. In my public report, I claimed that she stated to me she knew who our company was, and whom I was. She proceeded to inform me that she had been told we had no way of verifying overseas military, which was simply not true. We had already contracted with a company called ID.me, which would verify every member. Someone also told her that we had no way of paying for content, which was not entirely accurate. Did we have million's in our bank account in donations to buy content, no we did not. We were waiting to implement a donor drive for when we signed our first broadcasting agreement, which was our business model for funding content. When I told her what she was told was not true, and asked who told her this, she told me only that she had been contacted by AFN, and that AFN had told her all about us. It didn't take much for me to put two and two together.

Just then, it all started to make sense why the people we had such great conversations with at NATPE, were no longer returning our calls. But why would someone, anyone, at AFN wanted to call these major content distributors and tell them not to do business with us? It made no sense, and then the answer dawned on me. What was the motivation of pretty much all the fraud, waste, and abuse of authority I witnessed in the last decade? Money!

AFN has a roughly $100 million-dollar taxpayer funded budget (give or take a few million,) which purchases millions of dollars annually in content from these large distributors like FOX. Think about it, look how the NFL made millions in the recent "paid patriotism" scandals where they were getting paid to let the military do flyovers and holding flag events for veterans. The public was outraged, rightfully so, and the NFL was pressured into refunding the money to the Department of Defense. So, I am thinking either, A: these companies donate a little content, but are getting paid big bucks for these prime-time programs. Or, B: AFN is afraid that if these distributors can get a tax deduction for donating content to us, then why would they need AFN? Either of these scenarios is entirely possible to me, based on everything I have witnessed over the last decade. What other possible reason would AFN's director of TV have to gain? There was considerable risk that came with contacting these companies about a small veteran based non-profit like us, and you with think someone like a director would know this. I do strongly believe a government organization that is currently accepting contracted proposals to provide competing services to our veteran based non-profit, has no business trying to interfere. In my opinion, that could be a violation under anti-trust laws, just like if a company like Apple used their influence against a smaller competitor - Let alone doing it to a veteran based non-profit. I cannot believe Apple executives would favor the optics of a public relations nightmare scenario like that, but none of this seemed to bother AFN's director of TV.

I drafted a complaint detailing what had happened and sent it to the Inspector General with the Defense Media Activity, which is the governing organization that oversees AFN. A screenshot of the actual complaint is shown below, but a simple FOIA request to the DMA will provide an actual copy of the original as well.

Nearly all the fraud, waste, and abuse I have documented, shares so many similarities to what has been documented with the Clinton email scandal, and this chapter in my life is no exception. With the release (June, 2016) of the IG's initial response to the investigation request made into Hillary's email server, you can see the same obstruction and lack of cooperation from the IG which I experienced between AFN and FOX. You also see absolute contempt for following regulations, and the close relationships between government employees in leadership positions, and private corporations.

Hillary Clinton wanted to maintain the ability to communicate between personal and government from a single device. She has said this from the beginning, and there are ways to go about this which conforms to security protocols already in place to protect our national security. Snap Chat is a great way to communicate with friends, some business conversations, and terrorists, where the goal is to have no accountability or record that remains of private conversations. This is not the model we decided on for accountability within our government and FOIA. The current system appears significantly broken, but I believe it could work effectively and efficiently with only a few small tweaks in policy, enforcement, and support from our leadership. The biggest problem, which is quite simple to fix if we wanted to, is the lack of support for new technologies from our leaders at the directorate level up. What complicates things worse is that while the Defense Department is developing sensible and effective measures to protect the information and make it more accessible, our leadership simply feels significantly privileged enough to circumvent these measures. As I touched on briefly earlier, in one State Department cable, (State Department cable, June 28, 2011) Hillary instructs State Department employees not to use personal email for government business. I wonder if she had the gall to send this from her personal email account? That also begs another security vulnerability point in which, when you use multiple accounts from a single application or device, it is easy to accidently send from the wrong account. That is some hard toothpaste to be putting back in the tube once sent. A former colleague of mine helped to develop a system that was authorized to have two (2) classified networks on the same computer, but I cannot go into details. In virtually all the rest of the DoD, a computer or device which is classified as "Secret" or "Top-Secret," cannot physically touch the same computer or device with a lesser classification that itself. Classified documents can easily go up in their classifications, but not so easily go down. This policy was designed to prevent accidental spillage of classified information. I have seen with my own eyes direct evidence of Hillary's desire to use one (1) device, because she was not a computer savvy person, and didn't want to be juggling two (2) devices. Yes, in the age of technology and the constant threat of cyber terrorism, we certainly don't want our president to be a "computer savvy person." If that was the case, my 92-year-old grandmother would make a better choice to oversee our cyber defense, God rest her soul.

The majority of our government's emails are sent through a secure, yet unclassified network called the NIPR network. Almost all access to government emails on an unclassified network now requires CAC access and authentication. I was using my CAC to access government networks since I enlisted in 2005, and adoption of these higher levels of encryption happened quickly by government standards. CAC's, or Common Access Cards, authenticate using both a physical ID card that contains an encryption key, as well as requiring a password known only to the user. These encryption keys are entrusted strictly to authorized government and DoD networks like .mil or .gov. I would like to know if the emails Hillary was sending from her personal network servers, had a "trusted" security relationship with government CAC's? That was a joke, they didn't. It would be possible to partially accomplish this through request memorandums, but I haven't seen any evidence of this with the Clinton's private email server. In fact, as I understand, the IG report stated that no attempt to gain written, authorized permission was made by Clinton at the State Department. There were exemptions allowed at one time, but these policies change quite frequently, and I don't know if the specific policies in place would have allowed her to get approval for it back then anyway. I think it would have, but cannot be certain, and haven't heard anything publicly to answer this very important question yet. I wish that from a national security perspective, by someone that was responsible for securing government data for nearly a decade, they didn't allow these exceptions. Such exceptions inevitably create vulnerabilities in an otherwise secure network, even with the best of intentions.

Look closely at how the IG investigated my claims later in the book for whistleblower protection. Even though there were laws in place to protect contractors from retaliation when they come forward with credible information regarding fraud, waste, and abuse, I was somehow not protected. I didn't file the report to the IG for my protection, although I did believe I would have been protected based on the actual IG's website. I filed it to report fraud, waste, and abuse. To my knowledge, based on my conversation with the IG investigator, they looked at my claims and determined it didn't fall under 10 U.S.C. 2409 protections. None of the actual fraud, waste, and abuse I reported was ever investigated. This is why I have included it in my book, and I have no doubt from past experience that I will get in trouble for doing this, and the people I am actually trying to bring to justice won't even be questioned.

So back to my IG investigation into AFN. The IG opened an investigation and found the director of TV had in fact contacted at least one distributor, FOX Entertainment. When the IG contacted FOX asking them to answer some questions, FOX stalled the investigation for about 6 months and then refused to answer. Best guess why is largely because they don't have to. The IG doesn't have subpoena powers outside of the military. The IG closed the report siting FOX's refusal to cooperate as the reason.

Whistleblower Protection and Request for Investigation

DEPARTMENT OF DEFENSE
DEFENSE MEDIA ACTIVITY
6700 TAYLOR AVENUE
FORT MEADE, MD 20755-7061

PUBLIC AFFAIRS

OCT 1 9 2015

Patrick Bergy
Executive Director
MOPS Networks, Inc.

Dear Mr. Bergy,

This letter is in response to your March 3, 2015, letter to the Inspector General concerning alleged misconduct by Mr. Larry Marotta.

We conducted an inquiry into your allegations. The lack of cooperation from witnesses identified in your complaint letter, coupled with documentary evidence we obtained, resulted in insufficient evidence to support an inference of misconduct by Mr. Marotta.

This office will take no further action pertaining to these allegations, and this matter will be closed. If you have any questions, please contact me at (301) 222-6812 or via email at charles.w.marshall32.civ@mail.mil.

Charles W. Marshall
Acting Inspector General
Defense Media Activity

It is now April 2015. I had spent the last year on a contract that I know the government was paying at least $120,000 a year for me, plus administrative expenses to my company. I hadn't really done anything but watch movies and work on our veteran based non-profit. My program manager would make requests to J8 leadership every month or so to get guidance, and hopefully move forward on whatever the government decided they wanted to have done with the portal.

The Army had their Enterprise migration to the production version of the SharePoint portal in April of 2014. Although the previous J8 director loved what I had built for the J8 SharePoint portal, and the taxonomy I developed using the 10-1, COL McFadden and Dr. Knowles had scrapped it all - well over a years' worth of work and testing. We were told to just "stand fast" while they decided what they wanted to do. After the Enterprise migration in April of 2014, everything on our original site, and on the new site went to a "read-only" state. This made it so nobody could add or remove any content on our collaboration portal, just only read what was there already. It remained in that state for roughly the next year.

Then one day in April 2015, Dr. Knowles orders another GS working under him, David Scoffield, to request I provide Dr. Knowles with the exact same permissions I refused to give him roughly a year ago, because he didn't have the required memorandums for authorizing the access he was requesting. I said I would love to, Dave, just send me a copy of the required memorandums, signed by an O6 or above, as well as copies of the required certifications. I will submit to the A2NEC for approval, and they will get his permissions all setup. A year earlier when Dr. Knowles had gotten so upset, I filed a complaint for his threatening me. He had then gone around my back, used his position and authority, and found someone else that capitulated to him, and Dr. Knowles was granted the permissions he wanted on the government's unclassified network called NIPR. It was wrong, and violated regulations, but he seemingly only got it for the unclassified NIPR network. It would appear he was not so successful circumventing Army regulations to get access to the classified SIPR network. This is what he needed with the call from David, and it would appear he needed it right now. I politely and very professionally apologized to David and told him I could not grant Dr. Knowles escalated, administrative privileges on a military network classified as Secret, without the required documentation. It is not even something I control. There is a moment of silence, and then Dr. Knowles picks up the phone and starts yelling at me, screaming at the top of his lungs how I better just do this and stop fucking around and pissing him off, or I was going to regret it. My colleague, Justin Losh was sitting about 10 feet away and could hear him screaming at me over the phone. I then asked Dr. Knowles to give me a moment to confer with Justin to make sure I was not mistaken with the requirements, and Justin agreed with me.

After a few more threats and foul words, Dr. Knowles hung up. I immediately created an official complaint with my program manager detailing the entire incident, which Justin corroborated. Something was telling me this was going to be it, the final straw before they get rid of me once and for all. The next day my program manager calls me into his office and explains to me that based on Dr. Knowles recommendation to COL McFadden, still the acting J8 director, it had been decided the Knowledge Management position I had supported with USFK J8 for the last 5 years, was no longer needed. I was told that they were going to transfer J8's Knowledge Management requirements to the Public Affairs Office. The PAO didn't need a KM position, but rather they required a social media person. That person also required a bachelor's degree per the proposal request, which I didn't have. This action effectively terminated my position, and only my position, in a contract of around 15 people. The fact that the PAO position was for someone with a social media background would have made Justin, the other KMO on our contract, far more qualified than me. I even made this point in an email to our program manager, and to Jim Jones, the president of my company, Dynology. And yet they refused to have Justin take the PAO spot, and simply have me move in to fill the KM position Justin was doing. It is interesting how this all happens the day after Dr. Knowles threatens me for my refusal to violate Army and DISA regulations, and subsequent filing of a formal complaint, don't you think? I filed another more detailed complaint with my program manager, Buck Buchanan, requesting whistleblower protection to stop the modification of the contract they were doing to remove my position. In that official report, I quickly outlined much of the fraud, waste, and abuse that has happened since October of 2013, when the loss of data occurred. I wanted to make sure someone outside of Dr. Knowles, Col. McFadden, and Buck, knew how I have been punished ever since my original report by this small group of GS in our leadership. I stated that in my opinion, which is supported by facts, that they were now terminating me for refusing to violate Army security protocols. Additionally, I included in the official report the loss of my position by transferring my job to the PAO, where I did not meet many of the requirements. I felt this smacked of retaliation (or at least warranted closer review,) so I requested whistleblower protection, and demanded to my program manager that he send this request up the chain of command to the new deputy director, Mr. Kidd. At first, Buck refused on the grounds I did not submit it to him as a "formal" complaint, so I went back to my desk and added the word "formal" in front of the word complaint in the subject line, and sent it back to Buck. I have both emails, and they were just minutes apart, and the only difference is the addition of the word "formal" in the subject line. Both were sent to one person, my program manager Buck Buchanan, about two rooms down from my office. If you can suggest another alternative to my claim that I was forced to make it "formal" by my program manager, please let me know. If you cannot, this should suggest to you the resistance, not support, which I received from my command. I told him if he continued to refuse, I would take it directly to the IG. Not at all happy with this, Buck reluctantly emailed it to Mr. Kidd, whom I confirmed receipt the following week at our monthly J8 meeting. Mr. Kidd assured me personally that he was looking into this, and that he had sent it up the chain of command to the USFK staff level. A few weeks later I was asked to submit my resignation by Dynology, which I did. That said, I included that I was being forced to resign due to my position being moved to the PAO. I departed Korea on 29 May 2015 and headed to Washington, DC to begin laying the ground work for my non-profit organization. I felt that if I could make our veteran based non-profit successful, I would be able to actually do something with my skills for the troops, and get away from all the fraud, waste, and abuse of authority I have witnessed over the past decade. Oh, and for my reader's situational awareness, about a week after I had been forced to resign and flew out of South Korea, J8 changed their mind and decided not to move my position to the PAO after all. Our roughly $12 million-dollar contract was again modified, but this time it was modified back to the exact same requirements it had before I was forced to resign. Seriously, are you starting to understand why I am so angry that I have spent the last two years writing a book about what happened to me? It is simply remarkable to me that something like this could have happened.

Several months later I wanted to find out the status of the formal complaint I had filed with the J8 deputy, so I emailed Mr. Kidd. He was out of town that day he claimed, and would get me a status the following week. I waited two weeks and heard nothing, so I sent him another request. He then told me he had sent my formal complaint requesting whistleblower protection to the contracting office, and not USFK staff HQ like he had told me earlier. He clearly didn't send it to the Inspector General where I had assumed he was required to send it. I think this is where most any intelligent person would assume someone at the directorate level would take it. Why would anyone receive a formal complaint with such serious accusations of fraud, waste, and abuse, and do nothing with it? Especially when a seasoned contractor, vetted and entrusted with a Top-Secret clearance, has implicated the J8 leadership. The accusations go all the way up to the acting director, and you just let it sit on your computer and do nothing with it for two months? It even confused the folks in contracting months later when they just received it out of nowhere. Hell, if there was a formal investigation, the people in contracting would have been investigated as well due to the modification of the original contract. The claims of retaliation I made required contracting to sign off on modifying the contract. This makes them at best a witness, and at worst, it could potentially implicate them. Mr. Kidd was now the J8 director, and inline for promotion to SES, which is the civilian equivalent of a 1-star general. We were told that Col. McFadden had been diagnosed with cancer and was forced out as J8's acting director for medical reasons.

So, I gathered up all of the emails and evidence I had collected over the last year and a half or so, and filed a formal complaint with the DoD IG directly in Washington. I provided time stamped reports, as well as official complaints that included statements from others that were present. I am humbled and honored to have been given the opportunities I was given to help defend our nation. In the end, fraud, waste and, abuse within my chain of command is what killed me, not our enemy or a terrorist.

My career in contracting for the military industrial complex came to an end in May 2015. I sought protection as a whistleblower in a complaint with the Department of Defense, Inspector General's Office.

Here's what the final report states:

> *Dear Mr. Bergy:*
> *This is in response to the complaint you filed with the Department of Defense Hotline on September 30, 2015, alleging reprisal under Title 10, United States Code, Section 2409 (10 U.S.C. 2409), "Contractor employees: protection from reprisal for disclosure of certain information," implemented by Defense Federal Acquisition Regulation Supplement, Subpart 203.9, "Whistleblower Protections for Contractor Employees."*
> *You alleged that management officials reprised against you for making protected disclosures.*
> *Your former employer, Dynology, is a subcontractor to Engility, the prime contractor under a U.S. Army contract. Employees of subcontractors are not covered under the provisions of the version of 10 U.S.C. 2409 applicable at the relevant time.*
> *Based on the above, we have closed your case.*

The "protected disclosures" they were referring to were all well documented allegations of possible crimes and misconduct. None of the violations in DoD security protocols, fraud, waste, and abuse were even going to be investigated because it was reported by a sub-contractor, instead of someone employed by the prime on the contract. I guess it's all just ok, and never actually happened because it was reported by a sub, and not the prime, right?

Losing My Clearance

There are 3 types of clearances the government will issue. (1) Classified, which is good for 15 years. (2) Secret, which is good for 10 years, and (3) Top-Secret, which is good for 5 years. Previous assignments I held required a TS\SCI clearance, which is what I had when I came to Korea in 2010. My contract in South Korea only required a Secret clearance.

The cost to the government for renewing a TS is so high, I don't know for sure how my company ever justified to the government that I needed to maintain my TS clearance. What I do know is that a TS clearance is far more valuable to an employer than a Secret, for all the reasons I stated above. I was asked this question by our program manager wondering why my company was having the government spend so much money investigating a TS clearance that was not authorized or needed on the 5-year contract I was working in Korea. When I relayed his question in an email to the president of my company, Dynology, I could not find any response in my personal email archives from him with an answer, just the email I sent asking the question from my personal email account.

Preparing the background information for a Top-Secret clearance can take weeks, especially when you are 9,000 miles from your home. When you complete the form, it requires prior addresses you lived going back 10 years, including the names and contact information of people you lived with and your neighbors. Every place you have a stamp for that you visited in your passport needs to be accounted for, as well as anyone you cohabitated with, such as your wife, and her family. My company contacted me via email and said I had 24 hours to complete the background packet for a TS clearance, and if I didn't, my clearance would be revoked. Nothing like some good old advanced notice from your company's security officer, which in my case was Jim Jones, the president of Dynology and the son of Obama's former National Security Advisor. I freaked, and thought this was totally ridiculous. Nobody can properly complete their background packet in a week, even under the best circumstances, and I was in Korea.

Well, it was incomplete inaccurate, but I got it done in 24 hours and sent in to Jim after staying up all night working on it. I sent it off and thought everything was good. Jim acknowledge receipt, and said he would contact me with any further information he required. Remember, when you read what happens next, Jim Jones is the president of a company responsible for ensuring compliance with government issued clearances!

I ask all of those that question the intentions or integrity of General Flynn and anyone entering the new Trump administration to consider what is truly involved in completing a truly accurate e-QIP for a clearance.

I don't remember if at the time Dynology was in the process of moving to their new offices on the 15th floor, up from a lower floor in the beautiful Towers Crescent building in Tyson's Corner, VA., or what the reason really was for the screw-up. I was contacted a few months later with some new information on the status of my investigation. I was told that something went wrong and I had to replicate everything I put down in the previous background packet to a new one. It had to be as close to being exactly the same as possible, but that was going to be a problem, as I didn't have all of the original documents from November 2011. It was absolutely ridiculous, and I was told by Jim that my job depended on me having an active clearance, and if I didn't complete this in 24-48 hours, I would no longer have a clearance, or a job.

This time I was up over 30 hours straight getting this packet done for a TS clearance that I didn't even require, which the U.S. government ended up spending the next 4 years investigating. Talk about your "hurry up and wait" scenario. I completed it and literally ran to the Fed-Ex on base to send it out. The Fed-Ex truck came 15 minutes after I left for the last pickup of the week. You don't cut losing your job much closer than that. That is unless you actually had completed the form as it stated, and were not told by the president of your company, and the program manager, to falsify the dates.

On Feb 7, 2012, at 1:50 AM, "Patrick B. Bergy" wrote:

"Jim:

I got all documents out to you fed ex. literally ran over a mile to make it on time. Printed the last document and memo just 15 minutes to spare. I was very rushed on the memo. Even working on the docs last night after speaking with you and all day today. I essentially made exact duplicate of each document and signed them with today date. I only had one or 2 or the originals signed that I could find. I had sent you all my originals because I could not print well. I will check in a few others places and if I can find anything I will send them tomorrow. What I sent today is scheduled to arrive either Tuesday late or Wednesday. When I get back to my desk I will email you with all I did. I will work tonight on something better for a memorandum. I don't know if you need to send with an original signed copy or a digitally signed copy. If you need an original I will "send them tomorrow and will give you a Thursday delivery.

I spoke with Rich Blunt and asked him if MPRI had any issues getting an investigation done here in Korea. He said there are no issues and that OPM has both government and contractors here. Rich had a question though about my clearance that I could not answer. I received my TS in October, 2007 and is good for 5 years as I understand it for SBI. My job requires only secret and I understood secret is good for 6 or 7 years and doesn't require an investigation. What is the reason we are needing an investigation? He didn't care and is aware of the issue with the signatures and original copies after walking by my desk and seeing me working on them. Not something I brought up to him and again, he is fine with everything and offered to help if there was anything we needed.

Please send emails to my personal account for the time being. My Dynology email is not working correctly from my phone. It was working but I did not get your email from the weekend on my phone until I removed and reinstalled on my phone last evening. Works fine from my home and office computer though but I don't have the ability to check as frequently.

Regards,
Patrick

Wanting to make sure and cover my ass, I sent the above response to Jim Jones directly. In it I made clear how impossibly rushed I was to provide him with the documents. This process would normally take weeks to collect the information and properly complete. I was given 24-48 hours. And all of what I was rushing to do was just recreating the documents I did in a total rush back in

November. I don't know what the reason was for me having to re-do all of the documents from November, 2011, but it was now February, 2012, and I was being coerced with loss of my job to change the dates from February, which was the truth, to November, which was a lie. All because Jim lost the file I rushed to Fed-Ex him back in November.

As you can see in my initial email, I had redone all of the original documents from November, 2011 and signed them with today's date (February, 2012), just as the document required. This is a quote from the email shown above,

"I essentially made exact duplicate of each document and signed them with today date."

It really needed to be that way because I was signing a federal document that says it is a federal offense to knowingly provide false information, and this was knowingly false. The document was not originally created in November, 2011, it was re-created in February, 2012. I asked Jim in an earlier email to verify this was correct with the OPM, and followed the orders of my security officer, whom was also the president of Dynology. In fact, in my email you can see I mentioned that the OPM had refused the ones dated February 2012 and supports my concerns about what Jim can be clearly shown instructing me to do, and how he is getting frustrated with my reluctance to comply with his request.

I also brought to Jim's attention in my response a discussion I had with Ret. Brigadier General, Rich Blunt. This doesn't prove I spoke to Rich, whom was our program director, but it does prove that Jim Jones, the president of Dynology, was aware of this. His response that followed did not address any of the facts or questions I presented to him, but his response to this thread acknowledges his receipt. I also have emails that show I setup a phone meeting between Jim Jones and Rich. All I can say is that these are my words in this email in which I describe the events that occurred at the time, and that is a fact. I make no claim that shows Rich Blunt would have agreed or disagreed. What I was told is that getting authorization from the federal government requesting an investigation for renewal of my TS clearance on any job, whether the position only required Secret or not, would require someone from the prime on the contract (MPRI), to approve it. That someone would have to be at Rich Blunts level or above. A simple FOIA request will show exactly who from MPRI signed the document, as well as showing if they had stated a TS requirement for a position that only required Secret. I am very curious as to what their justification was. That said, whatever the justification, this investigation took nearly 4 years to complete, and likely cost taxpayers 10's, possibly hundreds of thousands of dollars to investigate. At no time did my contract in South Korea ever require me having a Top-Secret clearance. The reason for only having a clearance level equal to that of what your position requires is not just to save taxpayers a lot of money, which it does. It is also a matter of protecting national security by ensure people only are given the compartmentalized level of clearance they require at the time.

This was Jim's response a few hours later:

"Pat. You were to send signatures with Nov date. These are no good"

And I replied:

On Feb 7, 2012, at 7:10 AM, "Patrick B. Bergy" wrote:

"I sent both Jim. Should he ok but I only had 2 with the original signatures, and they are going to look exactly like the ones they are refusing. I sent the only originals to you in November. I have no means by which to send you originals signed and dated in November, only copies. I cleaned all documents up and could date them and sign them from October, but it would be obvious they were copies and clearly not signed then. Do you have the originals I sent before?

Please advise me as to how I should proceed. Can you speak to the contact with OPM for guidance?

Patrick

And Jim replied:

Subject: Re: eQip
Date: Tue, 7 Feb 2012 12:39:54 +0000
"Call now if u can"

I cannot verify what was said over the phone, so I will list only my response after our call:

Sent: Tuesday, February 07, 2012 8:07 AM
To: jjones@dynology.com
Subject: RE: eQip
"Jim:

Here are the copies I cleaned up. I know you are busy, but if you can find a few minutes to write what you think I should say (I will fill in dates and such), it will make sure that my memo expresses most precisely what needs to be said. If not no worries, I will get it taken care of and send out Fed-Ex tomorrow. Let me know if the files I have attached look acceptable. They are extremely closely formatted and I was very careful to make sure all the content is accurate.

At this point I have been up more than 30 hours straight trying not to lose my job because someone else didn't do theirs. Jim received the copies I sent him to review and replied as follows:

Pat...I really don't know how to say this...the copies you sent are dated Feb...your investigation was not submitted in Feb...it was 11-28-11. It is different and they will not accept. Why is this not sinking in? You are making this WAY too difficult.

The files are acceptable in that they are legible but AGAIN...you have signed it in Feb!!!! I have zero time to write the letter but if you simply did what you said you were going to do...you wouldn't need to.

You need to advise me on how you want to proceed. I'm frustrated and I believe we may have lost the window to reply.

You need to also understand that I can no longer hold you on a contract without an active clearance should they render you into a loss of jurisdiction classification again. This could happen as early as Friday of this week for non-compliance.

I'm sorry Pat but you've made an easy situation extremely difficult. You need to call me ASAP and don't stop until you get a hold of
me.
I will be out of pocket from 12-3:30 EST
Jim Jones

To me, changing the date on an official document is extremely difficult, even though I had both a retired general, who is our program manager, and the president of my company, whom is the son of President Obama's National Security Advisor, Gen James Jones, telling me it was OK. It still didn't feel right to me, which is why I asked Jim to check with OPM to make sure it was OK, and assumed it was. That is also why I put it in the email I sent to Jim, and had it sent to my personal email account. I figured someday if there was a problem and I lost my clearance, it wouldn't be just my word against theirs. That someday came, and I was correct in documenting it, but it didn't do me much good so far.

Aside from the fact my job only required a Secret clearance, I knew it was a horrible idea to run my Top-Secret clearance less than a year after my first divorce. Doing my Top-Secret wouldn't have been a bad thing, if I was given more than 2 days to complete a security packet that lists everything I have done and everyone I have known in the last 10 years. A complete and accurate packet is essential for adjudication of your clearance, especially if you have had any major changes in your relationships. Jim Jones was not just the president of my company telling me that if I didn't alter this document I would be fired, he was also my Security Officer, and was the one who instructs me on what to do. Jim knowingly submitted a falsified document to a federal agency that affirmed everything was true under penalty of law. I just did what my security officer told me, and documented everything. In the government, we call that CYA, or covering your ass.

There is no protection you can get from the government when something like this happens. If I don't do what my security officer tells me, and I have expressed my concerns, there is nothing I can do. Does anyone believe this abuse of authority is the exception, and not the rule? If you do, you are wrong! This has been the rule with every company since I started working for the military.

This was my response to Jim:

From: Patrick B. Bergy
Sent: Tuesday, February 07, 2012 5:22 PM
To: jjones@dynology.com
Subject: RE: eQip

"Jim. Those are the files I already sent you from work. I just wanted you to open and look at them to make sure they are acceptable, as

they are acceptable. other original and I spent the better part of 2 days reproducing them. Today, when I get to the office, I will print, sign with November date, scan and send to you Fed-ex by 3pm. You just were not able to open the Zip file I sent you so I opened and sent same file back. I fully understand you want the new files I created yesterday dated for November and signed now. You will have that shortly and the originals in hand Thursday.

    Patrick

And this was Jim's response to me:

jjones@dynology.com <jjones@dynology.com> wrote:

    "Pat...you need to call me. This is getting crazy. I only have one original with the 11-28-11 and that is the authorization for release of information and a copy of the fair credit reporting disclosure with the same date (not the original). Other items are dated 2-7-12 or have portions that are not readable. What gives? Is there another FedEx on the way...hopefully?

    Jim Jones"

*You will notice my comment in the above thread says **"I fully understand you want the new files I created yesterday dated for November and signed now."***

How can a document dated November but signed and created in February, swearing under penalty of Federal law that everything is true and accurate, be legal? My employer/security officer was telling me this was required, but I cannot imagine why it was ever necessary. I really wonder what happened between November 2011 and February, 2012 that required all of this to be done again. I don't remember what reason I was given exactly, but do know it wasn't because of anything I did. Once I completed my eQip in November, I gave it to my company security officer, and they are responsible for administration and management of my clearance. I want to say it was an administrative error that went unnoticed because Dynology was in the middle of moving their offices, but I cannot remember for sure. I do know I was being treated like garbage for something that was impossible to do, wasn't necessary, required falsifying federal documents, and was not the result of anything I had done wrong or caused.

    If the email thread I showed you above sounds like my TS clearance was sort of screwed from the beginning, you would be correct. Not renewing my TS and leaving me with having a secret clearance for the next 5 years wasn't good enough, even though that is all I required for the next 3 or more years that was left on my 5 year contract. I cannot speculate as to why my company would do this, I can only provide you with documented evidence in the form of emails from the president of my company that they did.

I can tell you that the value a TS clearance adds to an employee of a company is in the $10's of thousands of dollars annually. The correct process would be to let the TS expire, and if I did get a job that required a TS, my company would submit for an interim clearance and I would start the TS process over again at that time. I couldn't even guess at how much fraud, waste, and abuse like these costs taxpayers. This was my clearance, issued by the U.S. Department of Defense before I even began working for Dynology. My company is tasked only with managing my clearance, not managing their clearance so they could use to profit from on other bids.

I have detailed my email correspondence with Dynology to you as factual evidence for you to make your own conclusions. It is common knowledge that many companies use security-cleared employees with Top-Secret clearance to bid on projects that the employee will never even work on if they win the contract. All they want are security-cleared names on the proposal. The average salary of an IT person with a Top-Secret clearance is between $100,000 and $130,000 or more annually. Already having had a Top-Secret clearance makes the process much easier for someone like me after I leave Korea and take another clearance job that requires a TS clearance. Having my clearance administratively revoked makes it far more difficult.

General Jones and his son, Jim, now oversee a company that is responsible for compliance of government clearances. I have submitted a copy of this to the FBI, Inspector General, and my congressman, Charlie Crist, in hopes they will investigate, but I am not holding my breath. These folks represent the deepest depths of DC "deep state" swamp known as the Military Industrial Complex.

6   The Journey Home
My Journey to the Non-Profit Mecca - DC

My dog, Nikki, who is the cutest Chihawawa and Jack
Russell mix dog you have ever seen, flew with me back to the states.
I adopted her in Hae Bong Cheon, South Korea, in early 2013 as a
puppy. We arrived in Washington, DC with a small amount in
savings. I got an Airbnb, which is the cheapest place I could find in
DC for $2,000 per month. I couldn't get an apartment without a job
that showed a W2, and the work I was doing as a director for the
non-profit was all voluntary. I was trying to get MOPS Networks
off the ground, and was working to build it into a full-time position.
Dynology told me they didn't have any contracts they could put me
on. I had put about $15,000 in the veteran's non-profit over the past
year, prior to leaving Korea, and thousands of hours of my personal
time. Not to mention the time my three partners, Ed, Fred and Justin
had put into it. I wanted it to succeed more than anything. I wanted
to be a part of something good, something special, after having lost
my career to the rampant fraud, waste, and abuse I found in our
government.
   Microsoft had donated to our non-profit an E3 Enterprise
SharePoint portal and Office 365 with unlimited licensing, all for
free. Office 365 now had incorporated their Azure Media Services
into SharePoint and Office 365. Justin and I used our knowledge as

subject matter experts in SharePoint to build out a portal with a social media component, document libraries and drag and drop video. The IG investigation into AFN and FOX was closed, and AFN now had signed a multi-million-dollar deal with a large content provider to provide video on demand services to our troops overseas. This, to me, is outrageous, but there was nothing at this point I could do. When I was in Iraq and Afghanistan and my family was back home in the states, I was paying for licensing of prime-time content through my cable provider, and then paying for it again through AFN while deployed in defense of our nation in a combat zone. Why is it that with my cable subscription back in the states, I can travel anywhere in the U.S. and access my content online using my login through my cable provider, but not have that same licensing extended to me when I was deployed overseas serving my country? Our troops are paying twice for the rights to watch the same content. While our troops were getting screwed by paying twice for content, these content providers were waiving their flags and saying, "we support our troops." I personally see it as nothing more than paid patriotism. I submitted a freedom of information request to the Defense Media Activity for answers to what our government was paying these distributors for this paid patriotism. The FOIA request was made through the same organization that I filed my IG complaint with against AFN. My FOIA request was denied.

Remind You of Anyone (Hillary Clinton?)

Recently, as I am writing the final chapters of my book, the Inspector General (IG) release its findings into Hillary's email controversy. When the IG asked FOX Entertainment if there were any conversations between themselves and AFN, they seemed to acknowledge there was, but refused to answer any questions. This was mentioned in the final report presented to me as issued by the DMA's IG in my complaint against the Director of Television for AFN.

Now look, at all the claims I have made thus far with those in our leadership (like Hillary Clinton, USFK J8,) threatening anyone whom questions actions that are many times in very clear and direct violation of DoD regulations and policies. Reading what transpired in the State Department Inspector General's report is exact the exact same, just on a different day. This abuse of authority, which places our national security at risk, is a completely systemic problem. The trouble with fixing the problem is getting contractors to come forward. For me, looking back now at what Hillary said during her debate back in October 2015, I can't help but think what the reason could there have been for contractors not to have actually been protected. Hillary claimed during the debate contractors and sub-contractors were! Was not actually including contractors out of fear these contractors may come forward? Could it be to protect the abuse of power described in the State Departments IG report on Hillary's private email server, and likely other events we haven't even heard about yet? The same and even worse abuse of such authority goes back for decades, and all the way to the presidency in both democrat and republican administrations. Maybe this has something to do with why most people just don't seem to care, but I don't have such a luxury, as it has directly affected me since my decision to enlist.

When Congress passes a law intended to protect contractors that come forward to report fraud, waste, and abuse in our government, exempting all contractors that were on an existing contract serves only to protect those implicated in the official reports. As I understand it, and please feel free to correct me if I am wrong, private contractors employed by Hillary Clinton while she was Secretary of State would not be protected from retaliation if they came forward even today? The FBI had to give one contractor immunity from prosecution to provide testimony about Hillary's email server. Would this contractor, and others listed in the IG's report, have come forward when they were first threatened by Hillary and others in her State Department if they were protected? If they had, what we now know was a serious breach in national security by using a private email server, may have never happened. Just look at what happened to me in the previous section when I reported the PII incident involving Dwight Patton sending confidential information unencrypted on an unclassified network.

Like I have said repeatedly, these threats of termination to protect the contract and not upsetting the client were very, very, common. What was not common is having a program director say it in an email, allowing me to show documented evidence of my claims. Seriously, nobody cares this happened, or that I have documented evidence of it. My resignation from Leonie, and not pushing my official report of pornography with underage boys and old men in Iraq to the IG, is just the tip of the iceberg. I have suggested a potential Coup d'état earlier of a $10 billion-dollar military project, with total awareness of it happening. Fixing this systemic abuse of authority must start with holding our leadership accountable. Hearing Hillary deny having done anything wrong is not going to solve this problem, it only takes us deeper into it. Taking her clearance away will though. I bet taking Bill Clinton's clearance away years ago for having an affair would have gave others thinking of doing the same, second thoughts. I will say it again, it's the same standards that are applied to everyone else, and this is not a political position. The same applies to private contractors that have leadership positions, such as program managers. If they knew violating regulations to protect the contract would result in the loss of their clearance, I bet they would think twice before placing the contract above that of our national security. They know these rules now, but watching people like General Petraeus, the Clinton's, and others getting away with it, only serves to embolden them.

I believe one of the most serious things Hillary did was to send an email instructing one of her colleagues to remove the classified header at the top of the page. This is not made up, this email exists and is publicly available. Apparently, the person was having trouble sending the document labeled as classified, over an unclassified network. Understanding the problem here for Hillary is simple – don't send out classified information over an unclassified network unless you have removed all classified information, and then get authorization from a governing authority. Removing the "classified" header on the document you are sending, while leaving the actual classified information in the document, Hillary, is not what Defense Department policy requirements meant by not sending information marked as classified. If you attend a classified briefing, then go and repeat that information in an unclassified e-mail, you are wrong! You don't do that, it is illegal and you can go to jail. Hillary's excuse is that she never sent or received anything labeled as classified. Well of course she didn't, because as you can clearly see and read in her very words, she instructed at least one person to remove the classified header and send it with the classified information still in the e-mail. It is disingenuous for her to claim all her emails were classified later, after it was sent. You notice how Hillary NEVER says that she never sent classified information. What she says is that she never sent or received any emails MARKED as classified. If someone can show me even one instance publicly where she leaves out the word "marked," then I will publicly apologize, but I don't see that happening. Sending classified information on an unclassified NIPR network – with or without being marked classified, is ILLEGAL, and threatens our national security.

White lies do matter, and I personally think Hillary looks at her excuse as a little white lie. These white lies actually matter when you are talking about national security. Bill Clinton used a little white lie when he was president and being asked about Monica Lewinski. Imagine if nobody investigated Bill Clinton, and some foreign country hostile to U.S. interests were to have found out, something like that could have been used to influence our freaking president!!! For all intentional purposes, Bill Clinton should have had his clearance either placed in a loss of jurisdiction or suspended, pending the outcome of an investigation. But as I understand it, the president doesn't actually even have a clearance. What I am saying is simply what the rules say you do. These are the same rules most everyone else has to live by to ensure our national security, unless you're Petraeus, the president, or his wife.

I am not a small fish in a big ocean, I am freaking plankton. Metaphorically speaking, even small fish on a daily basis eat people like me up and poop me out. But that's ok because not all of the plankton (me/us) gets pooped out (metaphorically speaking,) some of what we were remains in the small fish, and makes that small fish a big fish someday. So, there you have a metaphoric example of how the food chain can be used to effect positive change in our government. If we feed our leaders with good information (good plankton,) and our president uses the best part of us, and poops out the metaphorical fraud, waste, and abuse, then the big fish cycle gets stronger and healthier. This is not achieved when someone like Hillary sends out an email to everyone - from her private email server (I say again, is in direct violation of numerous regulations,) telling them not to use their personal email accounts for official government business. I truly don't know what email account she used to tell people this policy, but it has been my experience that our leadership often becomes so out of touch, it wouldn't surprise me in the slightest if she did. This would be an example of what happens when a big fish (Hillary as Secretary of State) decides to just eat the poop floating close around them because they have gotten fat and lazy from all the free government bullshit that surrounds them. Eating the garbage they get paid to eat from lobbyists and corporations can make someone real fat quick. So, there you have it. I would consider most of my best efforts thus far to be at best (metaphorically speaking) resembling a healthy yet insignificant, farm raised and nutritionally balanced plankton.

McCain, Manafort; Connections to 2016 Russian False Flag

You must assume the words that come from a politician's mouth is simply BS until proven otherwise. Ignore this rule at your own fate! Understanding this, do you just accept John McCain's very public anti-Russian persona? It is not my intention to question the integrity of anyone in this post, but it is important to ask direct questions, and expect direct answers. Before dismissing what I am saying, know that I spent the last decade in the deepest depths of the DC swamp. I held an above Top-Secret clearance, and provided support at the highest levels of the U.S. Government, both in and out of uniform. I know how these people operate. There is nobody better to fight these people, then someone that has been a part of it. My career and life were destroyed after being let go because of having too much integrity to lie. Read the facts below and decide for yourself.

image #1 Tactical, Military Grade IIA for Social Media PSYOP

I went to work for Dynology Corporation in October of 2007. They sent me to Camp Liberty in Baghdad, Iraq in support of the Joint Psychological Operations Task Force (JOPTF) to develop pioneering technology in social media psychological operations (IIA PSYOP) and information operations (IO.) IIA, which stands for Interactive Internet Activities, was in its infancy at this time. (See IIA DoD definition at bottom of post.)

I cannot discuss what we did with the applications I helped in pioneering for the Department of Defense, or discuss anything to do with the dissemination process. There are 100's of potential uses for an application like this, both good and bad. Once it became an off the shelf product is where my background as an SME in social media psychological warfare begins to theorize potential threats.

We lost the Iraq contract the following year in a re-compete, but Dynology was somehow allowed to maintain the intellectual property rights for the application we were paid for developing by the Department of Defense. Appears to be the rule, not the exception but I don't understand how it would be allowed. "Image #1" above is an unclassified beta version snapshot of the iPSY application. Notice how it is capable of incorporating IO (anonymized, covert) with IIA to support tactical, computer network operations.

The defense department paid for the application to be entirely rebuilt by the company that won the re-bit and replaced us. Strangely, as you will read in my book, Victim of the Swamp, we discovered the new company didn't know the project had an IT component, required an IIA application or two full time IT guys. They told us this while trying to get us to stay on and help them. No wonder they won as the lowest bidders. Swamp is deep folks and I don't want to drift into an OTP. Still, it doesn't seem like the best use of taxpayer dollars by Obama's acting National Security advisor. I personally was tasked with producing the marketing slicks for commercial sale of this tactical social media psychological warfare application. This application can do many things. We called the retail beta version of the application iPSY. It can be used to help change the hearts and Minds of two warring factions, or in helping to move milk Off the Shelf at your local grocery store. The covert and anonymity capability are perfect for a Police Department to catch child Predators online.

Another thing it is capable of is altering the outcome of a presidential election. In fact, if those currently suspected of influencing the 2016 US elections were to have done it, they would require a project management tool with the exact same capabilities as what I developed for Dynology. There is an uncomfortably close relationship to ret. Gen. James Jones, Obama's National Security Advisor. Think of it as a project management tool for coordination/ dissemination for IO (hacking/malware/covert "false flag" operations,) and IIA, for social media psychological warfare.
This would include managing the narrative using fake blogs, websites and the Main stream media that any country or private project would have on their payroll.
Let that sink in for a minute, and continue reading for now.

Here is where it starts to get interesting. Quick recap; Dynology is a family-owned business that was founded by retired 4 star Marine General James Jones. With his son, Jim Jones, at the helm.

Dynology has bid on and won Millions in defense department contracts, many while General Jones was acting in an official capacity as President Obama's National Security Advisor!

I bet many other companies that sometimes spend hundreds of thousands of dollars if not more on bidding contracts would not be happy to find out they lost to a company that was owned by Obama's National Security Advisor. I think most will agree the potential for abuse is unacceptable.

The close, lifelong relationship between General Jones and Senator McCain is well documented. His son, Jim Jones, work his first job as an intern for John McCain. So we have this very well-documented relationship between John McCain, General Jones and Dynology.

Now enter Paul Manafort, the person listed in several articles, one being an article from The Huffington Post listed below, as a primary suspect in influencing the Ukrainian elections, as well as the 2016 elections here in the US. Paul Manafort's work with John McCain campaigns go back well over a decade. John McCain has thus far simply denied any knowledge of Paul Manafort and his work with the Ukrainian election in 2010. McCain's denial did not seem to sit well with the Huffington Post reporter, as McCain and Manafort shared an office during that time.
http://www.huffingtonpost.com/2008/06/20/new-questions-over-mccain_n_108204.html

Could John McCain have potentially organized a tactical IIA/IO that was designed to show collusion between President Trump, his campaign staff, and the Russians? McCain's lifelong relationship with General Jones, Obama's National Security Advisor, and the development of social media psychological warfare applications by Dynology, would suggest this is who John McCain would reach out to. As Obama's former National Security advisor, General Jones would make a powerful Ally with strong ties to the intelligence community. Dynology's technical capabilities and having people in place at the highest level in our intelligence Community would be required to accomplish what reports suggest Paul Manafort was involved with. With all the speculation going around regarding the Russian narrative, I've never heard anyone ask and answer the question of how they would do it? This theory goes a long way towards answering that very question. If true, it would likely provide investigators with a trail to follow the money. You

don't just wake up one day and decide to alter the outcome of the U.S. presidential election by calling The Geek Squad. These are covert, multi-million-dollar operations that require Battlefield tested applications, project managers and analysts. I am not a strong believer in coincidence, and thus far John McCain's excuse is ignorance.
Below is a link to the Google Way Back Machine snapshot of Paul Manafort's corporate website.
http://web.archive.org/web/20070304101901/www.3edc.net/partners/

If you're looking for the swamp, look no further than the relationship between our government, the military, and the military industrial complex. Contractors, like me, provide plausible deniability to our clients in the government. This is why military contractors are used so frequently comma and show up so often in situations like Hillary Clinton's email server, where the contractor was responsible for the server, yet so many emails were destroyed or missing. Clinton's system administrator plead the 5th during Senate hearings, and there was nothing in the law to go after him and compel him to answer. Contractors, contrary to popular belief, do not have protection under US whistle-blower laws. If a contractor did speak up, that contractor would ruin his career and his life. Believe me, I know this to be true from first-hand experience. My life in career was destroyed after coming forward with an official report of fraud waste and abuse. If we are ever to drain the swamp, we need to begin by providing strong whistle-blower protection to those who are willing to speak out, even at their own personal risk. We do not abandon these people or throw them under the bus, they are the only way we will ever drain the swamp.

7   EPILOGUE

Thank-you for reading, and hopefully sharing my story. I lost my home, my wife (actually three of them now), my family, and finally my career. I am reminded of a short time back, on my daughters 15th birthday, when exactly 10 years ago on that 30 October 2005, I was able to sneak out of basic training with the help of a drill sergeant, and make a call to my daughters, Mia and Sarah, on their birthday. It is one of many heartwarming memories, and some not so heartwarming. It for sure wasn't all bad, and I was so blessed to have been even a small part in this moment of history. To ignore the acts of fraud, waste, and abuse in our government, is nothing less than a victory for our enemies.

Over the last decade, what I witnessed was an extremely unhealthy relationship between our government and private military contracting companies, also known as the military industrial complex, MIC, and the swamp. With the money the Department of Defense spent on me as a contractor in Iraq for one year, they could have doubled the annual salary of ten E3's (Army Privates) and provided them each with an associate's degree. Not one single contract position I filled over the last 8 years couldn't have just as easily been filled by ten E3 privates, at double their normal annual salary. The Department of Defense spent north of two hundred thousand dollars to train and provide me with a Top-Secret clearance. When I enlisted I had a wife and two children, but shortly after we had twin sons. The salary for an E3 with a wife and four dependents was about $1,700 per month after taxes. Maybe a few hundred more depending on where I got deployed. While that E3 private deployed in a war zones struggles to make ends meet, he is surrounded by people, in many cases far less qualified than him, making $17,000 per month. Even more astounding is the contractor is paying no taxes up to the first $100,000. Our troops pay taxes when deployed overseas. How is that possible? So, guess what happens when that E3 private completes his service and is faced with either re-enlisting, and having his family living on food stamps, or go to work as a contractor overseas. The Top-Secret clearance our government just spent hundreds of thousands of dollars to get, is now being used by a private company on a contract our government is paying for. It is a system that is built to fail, unless you're a corporation in the military industrial complex, or a politician. Just think about those numbers. You want a way to cut our national debt? I bet that you could give our troops a 100% increase to their current salary, once they have completed a real college degree in their respective fields. The college would be military, and tuition is provided by the military. As our troops graduate in their respective fields, have them fill the positions currently held by private military contractors. Eventually we could be replacing likely 90% of the military industrial complex contract support, with soldiers. Adjust some of the PT requirements in certain non-combat, non-emergency essential, specialized fields or military occupational specialty. Oh, and get rid of the government civilians. If you want to work in the military, enlist! If you just want a job in the government, and you haven't served in the military, find one at the state level. Leave the federal jobs for our troops after their honorable service. The roll of our government is one of the most debated issues in current times.

One thing I believe a majority on all sides of this issue do agree on, is that the primary role of our government is for its military capacity to protect the freedom we have earned. The U.S. government has such a large military budget, yet our troops have the lowest level of education, and make such pitiful salaries. Our vets have staggering high rates of suicide, and I have seen firsthand the homeless veteran community. I can find out about anything to do with salary statistics and enlistment numbers with our military online, but cannot find anything that clearly and easily provides the same information on contractors. There is a reason why something that consumes so much taxpayer appropriated funding, is so difficult to find data analytics for. I have heard all the arguments for why we need so many contractors, and in my opinion, they are wrong. I think every woman and man should serve a mandatory 2 years in the military after their 18th birthday, and this would include even most people with physical disabilities. They work for little money, but are provided shelter, food, and uniforms, medical, dental and get a degree in the evening. After the 2 years is up, they can either leave and enter the economy for a job with a free degree, or re-enlist at a salary of at least twice of what it is today for a PFC in the Army. Heck, Bernie Sanders should love this idea with the free college! You could choose re-enlistment that is either emergency essential or non-emergency essential. Emergency essential would make more money, though. You could do everything I just said, and with what you save by cutting out the military industrial complex, I bet you would still cut the military's budget by double digits? Even better, with opportunities and really good benefits, you wouldn't need to require enlistment, people would want to enlist. Want to fix the illegal immigration problem, give the illegals a choice, if you're of military age, enlist for 5 years of service, or go home. After the 5 years of honorable service, you will go to the front of the line for citizenship, and so will your family. Anyone that has a problem with a veteran getting a visa, is wrong.

It is my opinion after spending the last decade witnessing the political process up close, my enlistment in the military and subsequent years as a contractor in the military industrial complex, that everything needs to be rethought.

I bore witness to the most worthless pool of government employees I could have ever imagined while working in South Korea, with only a handful of exceptions. And without exception, those that were not worthless, were prior military. In my personal opinion, even many of those that were prior military, had become so complacent in their roles as GS employees, that they had lost the edge they once had. I would likely blame that on the constant, well, bullshit that they had to put up with in our leadership, like with Regina Adams, the J8 deputy director. Regina never wore a uniform, yet was leading the J8 transformation, a multi-billion-dollar reconstruction project moving bases all throughout Korea to a single base south of Seoul.

I have to stop for a moment and tell a story here about what we were actually doing in South Korea. It would be funny, if not so sad. Let's do a little basic geography lesson here. North Korea is the enemy, and Seoul, a city of more than I believe 25+ million people, is about 80 or so miles south of North Korea. We are spending billions of dollars on a massive military base realignment, moving most of our troops just south of Seoul. So, if North Korea ever did attack, what direction do you think everyone in Seoul is going to evacuate, would they head north? I don't think so. I am pretty sure if North Korea attacks, and that is our entire reason for being there, then all 25+ million people in Seoul, are heading SOUTH. Now remember, all of our troops are SOUTH of Seoul. That means in the event of an attack, the $10 billion dollars we spent on a massive military installation SOUTH of Seoul, is going to be sending all of our troops NORTH, into a sea of 25+ million people - going SOUTH!

There was a small town with a church that sat smack dab in the middle of the land where Camp Humphries is being built (South of Seoul). That community of several hundred Koreans had refused to move, and the members of the community, along with thousands of others that came from around Korea, chained themselves to buildings in protest. The Korean government, with obviously no objections from the U.S. State Department led by Hillary Clinton, or it never would have been allowed to happen, came up with the idea to resolve the problem of the protesters chaining themselves to the church, by leveling everything else in this town to the ground. There, problem solved. No buildings, nothing to chain themselves to. Thousands of Koreans came out to protest, and the Korean government came in with literally thousands of police. It was a despicable act, and U.S. officials did nothing to stop it, or they would have.

We had some really good, smart people, like SES Parker, whom was a retired COL that had spent years serving in Korea prior to becoming the directory of J8. We had some good contractors that were analysts' onsite being paid a fortune. Our housing allowance alone was around $4,000 per month. With only a very few exceptions, the contractors could have done all of the work they did from stateside, and used VTC's (video tele-conference) to attend meetings. David Scoffield was a retired LTC that came to Korea as a contractor, and then took a position as a GS. This guy represents the best taxpayer money our country has ever spent. Then you have Dr. Knowles. I don't know if he has any military background. It would really surprise me if he did, because he fits perfectly into the mold I described as everything that is wrong with our government. There was a huge, multi-million-dollar battle simulation contract in Korea. Do we need to have this battle simulation in Korea, or could we have military there to maintain the network, and host this in a virtual cloud environment from stateside? Every year in Korea we had what was called UFG. It was a two-week training exercise where about 25 retired general officers would come too Korea for those two weeks, and get something like $1,000 per day to just sit and watch the exercises. I could be wrong with that number, I think it is actually higher, and the whole thing has become a big scandal in Korea, but I bet few stateside has ever head of it.

I didn't need to be in Korea, Iraq, or Afghanistan as a contractor. My primary job was SharePoint, which I could have administrated from ANYWHERE in the world other than where I was at. The military has IMO's on the ground in the event there was a physical connection problem with systems locally, if I couldn't access the servers remotely. In my 8 years as a contractor, the contracts I worked on never had more than 10-15 contractors working any one given contract. In that same 8-year time, taxpayers likely spent well north of half a billion dollars to fund these few small contracts I worked on. In that time, there might have been 5 positions that actually required a physical presence. Not on each contract, I am talking during the entire time I was in contracting, and everywhere I deployed. Maybe one or two people max would have been necessary to support the entire Korea contract with a physical presence. In Iraq, we didn't need anyone there. In Afghanistan, we had a handful of local nationals that needed to be there and maybe a program manager to coordinate on the ground with the military, but nobody else. Almost everything was done from within the confines of our base. So, if they never had to leave the base, and everything they did was online, why in the hell did they need to be there? Think about the hundreds of contracts just like the ones I worked on that were also being funded, but didn't need a physical presence. We need people on the ground to collect intelligence, support surveillance, and provide reconnaissance missions. Any analyst position that has a person on a contract that never leaves the base, and their sole mission is to analyze data collected from ISR, could all be done stateside and in real time. IIA programs could almost entirely be operated stateside, leaving our trained military, state department and other federal agencies on the ground in the combat zones executing missions, just like they do now to act on the data provided by the analysts.

To these large military corporations, it isn't about our national security, it is about money, plain and simple. Our presence there as contractors only complicated matters, and the officers and enlisted people that were making nothing compared to these contractors were all just thinking about how nice it will be when they get out of the military and can go to work for a big contracting company. I am guilty of that as well. But the grass is always greener on the other side, right. This problem would be solved by actually paying our brave men and women even half of what a contractor makes. A private stationed in South Korea takes home about $1,000 or less after taxes each month, yet I am making $6,000+ in salary each month, and a housing allowance of $4,000. How some stupid jerk like me is making ten times more every month, where the first $100,000 of it is tax free income, is impossible for me to even wrap my head around. I understand what they are thinking. I had a wife and 4 children to provide for. I am a patriot and I love my country, but how could I support them on less than $2,000 per month? It is largely my fault, because when I enlisted, I didn't have any idea of how little I would actually make. All I thought about was wanting to serve my country, and if my country would have actually provided me a salary that was even ¼ of what I was making as a contractor in Korea, or 1/8 of what I was making while in Iraq, I would have stayed. Oh, and if they could have been a little more flexible with the PT requirements as well.

We need to just get rid of nearly 90% of all overseas contractors, and pay our troops with the money we save. Oh, yeah, and give the foreign earned income exemption for up to $100,000 tax free now going to contractors, give that exemption to our troops instead! When I was in Afghanistan and my leadership was telling me to take out a low interest loan because they couldn't pay me a measly salary of about $1,000 every two weeks, and the contractor sitting next to me doing the exact same thing was making nearly $20,000 per month. Not to mention what that contractors company was making on the contract, which is often equal if not more than what the actual contractor is making. Do you understand how this undermines our military's ability to maintain quality soldiers?

When I joined the military, I had a wife and two children. Shortly after basic training my wife became pregnant with twins. My salary in the states on active duty orders was less than $2,000 per month even with a basic allowance for housing. Our mortgage alone was half of that. What was I supposed to do, put my family on welfare? In 2005 there were not a lot of people stepping up to the plate to serve in our military, and I am proud of my decision to enlist. But my government that I was fighting to defend was not stepping up for me or the other troops, but they sure were stepping up for the military industrial complex. I went from $2,000 a month or less after taxes in uniform in Afghanistan doing a hundred times the work I did in Iraq as a contractor, and they even screwed that up, asking me to take out a low interest loan in a combat zone. In Iraq I was making $20,000 per month, more than half of which was literally tax free, and in all of the spare time I had taking care of 7 brand new laptops, I took online courses at Saint Petersburg Collage. The education and training I got at Fort Gordon was the most bullshit and dysfunctional organization I have ever seen. The most common phrase used by nearly every instructor was "don't ask so many questions, you will learn this when you get to your unit." These were Cisco networking classes they were teaching, and nobody at my unit knew shit about it. Why aren't we providing our troops with a proper education during the 18 to 40-week courses being taught at Fort Gordon? I am talking about every single soldier leaving Fort Gordon with at least an associate's degree, with properly trained teachers and a college like atmosphere. Would 6-12 more months of full time education for everyone once they have successfully completed basic training be a bad thing for our military? I don't think so. You could do all of that and still pay them a minimum of $30,000 per year tax free for a fraction of what our government is spending on contractors.

I am told our government spent over $70,000 on my Top-Secret clearance, and then drove me out of the military six months after my clearance was approved because of ridiculous PT requirements meant for someone half my age, and a salary that is less than what McDonalds pays, even if you factor in housing, medical and food the military provided.

Thank-you for taking the time to read my story. Whatever we do, we can't keep doing the same and expect different results. America needs to have an "Awakening" just as we put together in Iraq. Our country has never been more divided, and if the Sunni and Shia can come together to fight a common enemy, so can Democrats and Republican's that share the same love for their country. The same type of social media psychological warfare applications I developed in Iraq, are being used right now to destabilize America and divide us. Knowledge is power, and we need to educate American citizens about what is happening. That is the only way we will win!

The End...

The image below is a letter of recommendation I received from the IIA Chief in Iraq. I included it to help in supporting my claims.

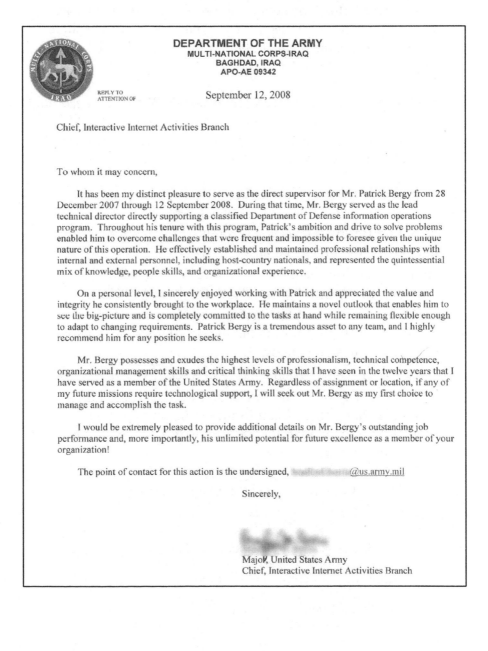

DEPARTMENT OF THE ARMY
MULTI-NATIONAL CORPS-IRAQ
BAGHDAD, IRAQ
APO-AE 09342

REPLY TO
ATTENTION OF

September 12, 2008

Chief, Interactive Internet Activities Branch

To whom it may concern,

It has been my distinct pleasure to serve as the direct supervisor for Mr. Patrick Bergy from 28 December 2007 through 12 September 2008. During that time, Mr. Bergy served as the lead technical director directly supporting a classified Department of Defense information operations program. Throughout his tenure with this program, Patrick's ambition and drive to solve problems enabled him to overcome challenges that were frequent and impossible to foresee given the unique nature of this operation. He effectively established and maintained professional relationships with internal and external personnel, including host-country nationals, and represented the quintessential mix of knowledge, people skills, and organizational experience.

On a personal level, I sincerely enjoyed working with Patrick and appreciated the value and integrity he consistently brought to the workplace. He maintains a novel outlook that enables him to see the big-picture and is completely committed to the tasks at hand while remaining flexible enough to adapt to changing requirements. Patrick Bergy is a tremendous asset to any team, and I highly recommend him for any position he seeks.

Mr. Bergy possesses and exudes the highest levels of professionalism, technical competence, organizational management skills and critical thinking skills that I have seen in the twelve years that I have served as a member of the United States Army. Regardless of assignment or location, if any of my future missions require technological support, I will seek out Mr. Bergy as my first choice to manage and accomplish the task.

I would be extremely pleased to provide additional details on Mr. Bergy's outstanding job performance and, more importantly, his unlimited potential for future excellence as a member of your organization!

The point of contact for this action is the undersigned, ~~~~~~~~~~~~@us.army.mil

Sincerely,

Major, United States Army
Chief, Interactive Internet Activities Branch

Acknowledgements

I wanted to end my story with acknowledging a few very special people that have helped me get through some very difficult times. Others mentioned here are just those that have been very positive influences. I can't name them all, but a few deserve special mention.

To my children, Mia, Sarah, Bruce, and James. What can I say but I am so very sorry for not being there for you as a father should outside of anything financial. I spent two years writing this stupid book largely for you, so you must know how much I love you.

My sister, Linda Bergy. What a pain I was to you as a brother growing up. Still, when I needed someone, you were there for me.

My sister Lori Bergy. I miss you and think of you often. Heaven is for sure much more organized now.

My friends, Todd Johnston, Javier Benevente. My craziness has never deterred our friendship, and I am deeply grateful.

My friend, Kevin Holly. When nobody would help get my message to the world, you stepped up and put me on your show. That was important, and you should know it!

To Chuck Carter, you've been a jerk. Let's see if you were right?

Lastly, Fredrick Taylor, a true Patriot and war hero, and Larry Roach, retired Navy, sheriff, and former father in law. You guys were both a great inspiration for me. My words cannot do justice to how much I mean that!

APPENDIX – NOTES AND SOURCES

(State elections chief: No cheap deals for touchscreens, n.d.)
http://miamiherald.typepad.com/nakedpolitics/2007/10/state-elections.html

(Bound for boot camp, he's booted from his job, 2005)
http://www.sptimes.com/2005/10/27/Hillsborough/Bound_for_boot_camp__.shtml

(State Department cable, June 28, 2011, n.d.)
http://www.foxnews.com/politics/interactive/2015/03/05/state-department-cable-june-28-2011/

Made in the USA
Columbia, SC
06 April 2021